FINANCIAL STRATEGY
FOR
HIGHER EDUCATION

A Field Guide for Presidents, CFOs, and Boards of Trustees

Michael K. Townsley, PhD

ISBN: 978-1-4834-1180-4 (sc)
ISBN: 978-1-4834-1181-1 (e)

Library of Congress Control Number: 2014908259

Lulu Publishing Services rev. date: 09/25/2014

Contents

LIST OF TABLES

Acknowledgments

I wish to acknowledge the support, assistance, and guidance of the following professional associates who helped me prepare this book. Dr. John Stevens, president of Stevens Strategy, has given me the encouragement and the resources to complete my work. He has been most generous with his time and his wisdom. Mr. Brendan Leonard, senior vice president of Stevens Strategy, has given me tremendous insight into strategic insight and planning based on his long experience in strategic and management planning. Dr. Debra Townsley has also provided many useful suggestions for the book that are based on her experience as a successful president of two private institutions. She has also encouraged me in my work and provided me the solace and the time to pursue this book.

Information about Stevens Strategy and Author's Biography

Stevens Strategy—Publication Sponsor

Stevens Strategy Website: http://www.stevensstrategy.com/
Stevens Strategy Services Statement:

Stevens Strategy is a full-service consulting firm specializing in managing the process of strategic change in colleges, universities, and schools. The Stevens firm offers professional services to the leaders of higher education institutions in the areas of strategic planning, strategic governance, focused strategic analysis, financial analysis and planning, and institution-wide policy development. Stevens' consultants have extensive experience serving higher education—including positions as present and former trustees, presidents, vice presidents, and other senior staff—each with a particular area of expertise in leadership and management. Their clients include independent and public institutions from the largest universities to the smallest colleges and schools in America and around the world.

Contact Information: John Stevens, president: jstevens@stevensstrategy.com

Michael Townsley, PhD: Biography

Dr. Townsley is a senior consultant at Stevens Strategy, where he has provided financial strategies and forecasting systems for many private institutions on the East Coast.

Dr. Townsley was the special assistant for finance, the dean of undergraduate studies, and a professor of business at Becker College. Before his time at Becker, he was the president of the Pennsylvania Institute of Technology. While there, he implemented a strategic redesign of the curriculum to respond to major changes in the Institute's student market. The plan also incorporated new marketing plans that applied tactics to reach out to new student markets.

Townsley was the senior vice president for finance and administration for Wilmington College for twenty years. There, he was the chief financial officer with additional responsibility for marketing, information systems, and off-campus sites. As senior vice president, he crafted and implemented a financial turnaround strategy that eliminated deficits and provided the financial framework to build one of the fastest growing private colleges in the Mid-Atlantic region.

Dr. Townsley has authored *Weathering Turbulent Times* and *The Small College Guide to Financial Health: Beating the Odds*, which are recognized for their insights into higher education by presidents, chief financial officers, members of boards of trustees, and government agencies. He also developed electronic books and reference guides for NACUBO, such as *The Financial Toolbox for Colleges and Universities*, *Strategic Turnarounds*, and *Debt—Investment Strategies*. He has published widely and made presentations at national conferences on financial management, strategic management, and other major issues facing colleges and universities.

Dr. Townsley holds a PhD from the University of Pennsylvania; his dissertation analyzed the impact of market share on pricing in higher education.

Contact Information: Michael Townsley, PhD: <u>mtownsley@</u> <u>stevensstrategy.com</u>

Preparing for Today's Financial Challenges

The fast-paced dynamics that are reframing the historic structure of higher education will force many private college and university trustees and presidents to make major changes in their financial strategies, budgets, and operational plans if they expect their institutions to survive. Pressure to change is coming from student markets, governmental regulations, technology, and new forms of competition. As higher education moves toward a quasi-for-profit model of financial management, the governance system of institutions remains fraught with ambiguities that will confound the speed and financial methods needed to respond to massive changes taking place. The following "Major Issues" pose significant concerns for private colleges and universities.

MAJOR ISSUES SHAPING THE PARADIGM SHIFT IN HIGHER EDUCATION

1. Debt and liquidity will continue to be problematic as colleges confront declining enrollments, new regulations, and tougher competition.
2. The economy, regulators, and accreditors will reshape higher education by demanding:
   a) A broader financial perspective rather than simply managing net income
   b) Economic equilibrium in institutional financial strategies
   c) Financial metrics for more control over financial condition
   d) Regulations that will define financial condition by limiting tuition increases
   e) Institutions to be held accountable and liable for a broader range of financial decisions.

It appears that these changes will push private institutions away from a purely nonprofit model and toward a for-profit model in which cash flow, asset growth, profit (surplus revenue), and management ratios will govern capital markets and the survivability of these institutions. These changes will take a toll on the relationships among the president, board of trustees, and accrediting commissions. As this new era matures, the financial management of higher education will change dramatically.

Given current challenges, negotiating through a maze of interests makes strategic planning a task that is fraught with frustration. Nevertheless, boards, presidents, and chief financial officers (CFOs) will be held responsible for not coming to grips with the consequences of changes in the character of higher education. Private and public agencies are not receptive to explanations that colleges are unique institutions because of their dual governance systems that divide authority between the academy and the administration; and therefore, little can be done but to preserve the *status quo*. Government and accrediting agencies are easily discomfited when they see the tidy little financial world demanded by their statutes or regulations muddied by a system of dual governance. As a result, the leadership of private institutions needs to be prepared to address how to make the following changes during the paradigm shift in higher education that is becoming more evident.

1. Develop no-frills colleges that minimize costs and limit increases in tuition rates.
2. Unlock the value inherent in their asset-liability structure to increase their financial resources.
3. Use endowments to produce predictable revenue streams to avoid huge realized or unrealized losses that cause large deficits.
4. Update IT to increase the availability of students to administrative, business, and student services.
5. Redesign the chart of accounts so that revenue-producing centers have reports showing their net revenue.
6. Find partners to cut the cost of delivering student, auxiliary, instructional, and administrative services.
7. Use financial flash reports presenting critical financial performance measures for the president and chief administrative officers.
8. Evaluate new programs using a revenue-centered model[1] to measure the probability of large, small, and zero paybacks.

Private colleges and universities, regardless of their trepidations about change, need to start now to develop strategic and operational plans before they are left in the dust by their competitors. The purpose of this book is to provide presidents, chief financial officers, and finance committees with a financial management handbook to guide their financial strategies and operational plans.

STRUCTURE OF THE FIELD GUIDE

Stevens Strategy believes that private institutions will need the best information to deal with the massive economic, financial, market, and regulatory changes that threaten their capacity to deliver on their missions. The company has put together this Field Guide to provide

---

[1] A revenue-centered model allocates administrative and support costs to centers that generate revenue.

boards, presidents, chief financial officers, and chief administrative officers with research, insights, and analytic tools. The chapters include nearly two decades of experience working with a broad range of private colleges and universities. The basic themes for each chapter and the appendices follow:

Chapter 1: *Financial Paradigm* offers a new method of managing the financial condition of an institution by encompassing all components of its financial structure.

Chapter 2: *Strategic Financial Paradigm* provides a model for achieving and managing financial equilibrium, which is the point where financial resources are able to sustain the mission of the institution.

Chapter 3: *Measuring Financial Health* describes several models for measuring the financial condition of an institution and for developing strategies to strengthen financial health.

Chapter 4: *Forecast Modeling* indicates the parameters needed to design a sophisticated budget forecast model.

Chapter 5: *Price and Discounts* discusses the requirements to effectively price tuition in highly competitive markets and in response to potential government regulations.

Chapter 6: *Cost and Operations Performance* lays out methods for analyzing and managing operational costs.

Chapter 7: *Dashboards* explains how dashboards can deliver important data needed to understand and manage operations at all levels in an institution.

Chapter 8: *Salient Relationships* discusses the network that needs to be created within an institution to assure that it achieves its strategies and carries out its operational plans.

Chapter 9: *Financial Management of Online Programs* considers budget development and management of online programs.

Chapter 10: *Field Guide Final Notes* pulls together the commentary and recommendations of the previous chapters.

Appendix 1: *Due Diligence* is a checklist of major items to consider when assessing operational performance.

Appendix 2: *Diagnostics* is a checklist that an institution can use during the assessment of the five major components of its structure: governance, academics, markets, finances, and management of operations.

Appendix 3: *Variable Budget Report* provides a format for analyzing variable revenue and expenses during the fiscal year to determine whether the institution is meeting its operational budget goals.

Appendix 4: *Strategic Options for Struggling Colleges* offers colleges several options for improving their financial conditions.

Appendix 5: *Sample Composite Financial Index Template* is a basic template to compute the composite financial index.[2]

Appendix 6: *Responsibility-Centered Management Model* has the basic rules for computing a responsibility centered matrix.

Appendix 7: *Dashboards* suggests a variety of dashboards for the president and chief officers of the institution.

Stevens Strategy believes that this <u>Field Guide</u> will provide you with perspectives, strategies, and methods that Stevens Strategy and others have successfully implemented at colleges and universities across the United States.

---

[2] Users should check with the latest editions Salluzzo, R. E., Tahey, P., Prager, F. J., and Cowen, C. J. (1999) *Ratio Analysis in Higher Education,* Washington DC: KPMG and Prager, McCarthy & Sealy.

Chapter 1

Strategic Financial Management Paradigm

Strategic Financial Management Paradigm

Financial strategy at most colleges and universities, especially private institutions, is simply a balanced, current operating budget. A single-year net income goal is outdated and dangerous because it ignores liquidity (cash flow), capital investments, and long-term operational controls. Too often a balanced budget is an artificial goal that fosters a piecemeal approach to strategy because it ignores systemic problems that are not confined to a single year or that cross other segments of the financial structure, such as cash, endowment performance, debt, deteriorating buildings and equipment, collapsing student markets, and competitive cost pressures. Financially-weakened institutions that focus solely on operational annual budgets will compound their financial problems over time and increase the cost of resolving their inherent weaknesses.

The annual operating budget is a weak tool for operationalizing a financial strategy because the development process can overwhelm financial strategy as budgets are substantively altered by internal politics, current circumstances, and unexpected events. College budgets must acknowledge that financial markets will remain unpredictable, that large demographic shifts will distort student markets, that government regulations will limit budgetary discretion, and that internal inflation rates will continue to drive up operational costs. Gone are the days when colleges could simply focus on a balanced budget to maintain financial viability. Colleges must have a broader vision of financial strategy, which encompasses cash balances, tangible assets, financial investments, debt, and income flows.

For an institution to utilize its resources to serve its mission and respond to economic change, the concept of the budget needs to be redefined. The budget should include more than the operating budget; it should also incorporate budgets for cash flows, capital investments, and capital asset management. Strategic financial management requires an explicit delineation of goals for the statements of activities, financial position, and cash flow. In addition, the budget should do more than establish annual estimates—it should be expanded into a multiyear budget. By encompassing the full panoply of the financial resources of an institution, it is able to bring more resources to bear when it develops new strategies. This aspect of the strategic financial management paradigm is most useful to struggling colleges that are long on assets and short on cash or credit capacity.

Besides the usual budget goals and estimates, the strategic financial management paradigm should include metrics to assess strategic, budgetary, and operational performance. Typically, a financial metric is a ratio or single factor that is an accepted indicator for measuring financial performance or depicting desired performance goals. A well-designed metric is both a tool for assessing performance and a portal for targeting performance strategies.

STRATEGIC FINANCIAL MANAGEMENT PARADIGM: ASSUMPTIONS, PURPOSE, GOALS, AND PRINCIPLES

Before work on a financial strategy begins, the presidents and chief administrative leaders need to assess the financial condition of the institution, preferably over a five-year period. The assessment identifies short and long-term operating and financial strengths and weaknesses. Financial strategies and plans (or a plan) will necessarily flow from a thorough and deep performance assessment. The structural elements of the strategic paradigm are set out below:

Purpose of the Financial Management Paradigm

The purpose of the paradigm is to guide the development of financial strategies and operational plans that will achieve economic equilibrium. (Economic equilibrium posits an economic state in which an institution of higher education has sufficient quality and quantity of resources to fulfill its mission.)[3]

Goals of the Financial Paradigm

1. Produce sufficient financial resources to:
   a. Maintain the purchasing power of its financial assets.
   b. Keep its facilities (buildings, furnishings, equipment, and technology) in satisfactory condition.

2. Manage:
   a. Current income flowing from enrollment, donations, and grants in order to generate positive changes in net assets that maintain the purchasing power of cash and endowment investments to keep its facilities in satisfactory condition.
   b. Investments to assure a stable endowment draw, to expand endowment principle for future generations of students, and to minimize the impact of losses on operations.
   c. Debt to expand revenue producing capacity of the institution.
   d. Fixed assets by monetizing assets no longer critical to the institution or assets whose value could be monetized to contribute to new strategies.

---

[3] See the chapter on "Economic Equilibrium" for further information.

Assumptions—Undergirding Core Principles

The general principles of the paradigm are based on these assumptions: (1) colleges must efficiently use all sources of wealth and monitor the allocation of its scarce resources to accomplish its mission; (2) the president and chief administrative officers must have the skill and understanding of the dynamics of their institution and the higher education market to effectively use the principles that make up strategy-driven financial management.

Financial Paradigm Core Principles

Principle One: Manage income flows from current operations(enrollment, donations, and grants), which is dependent on 1) developing new programs, redesigning existing programs, or eliminating revenue programs that do not support allocated costs; 2) new marketing strategies, and 3) expecting donations to exceed cost of gift campaigns.

Principle Two: Manage income flows from investments; set goals for investment returns in excess of the endowment floor; change the mix of investments to achieve investment goals;[4] set performance benchmarks for each class of investments; allocate investment principal among competing firms; and write an investment policy statement

---

[4] Two examples will show the intent of this principle. First, a portion of the investment mix must be sufficiently liquid to support cash demands of the college under normal conditions and under economic downturns. (For example, the portfolio should be sufficiently liquid that 25 percent of budget expenses could be quickly withdrawn in the event of an unexpected financial crisis.) Second, if the strategic model forecasts a series of deficits during the next five years, then the senior administrators should carefully evaluate how the current financial structure could be restructured to generate significant reserves for new initiatives that could eliminate the deficits.

Principle Three: Manage fixed assets by separating them into two categories as contributing or not contributing to the value[5] of the institution, and then determine if assets not contributing value to the institution (such as land, buildings, or equipment) could be sold, leased, or used for other purposes.

Principle Four: Manage debt service so that these payments are not affected by more than a twenty-five percent shortfall in annual revenues.

Principle Five: Set up a strategic initiative fund to support the development of new revenue sources or to make major expense reductions. The fund can remain within investments but should be sufficiently liquid to permit withdrawal within thirty days of the demand for investment funds. The fund should invest in projects that generate the largest net present value among the set of project options.

Financial Paradigm—Leadership, Forecasting, and Budgetary Principles

Principle One: Successful management of the financial paradigm requires board support of the president and a president with the wisdom and dynamism to determine the direction and magnitude of change. The board must insist on action, and if the current administrative staff cannot do the job, new administrative leadership is needed immediately. The board must be willing to pay for good leadership; mediocrity may save money, but it does not breed success.

Principle Two: The board of trustees should seriously consider the use of consultants when new strategic and operational plans are required. Too often consultants are seen

---

[5] Contributing to the value of the institution could be defined in something other than financial terms, such as their cultural or historic value.

as a drain on scarce cash. However, a reputable consulting team can often speed up change and take the heat off the administration as change is tested and introduced.

Principle Three: CFOs must be grounded in the accounting principles that govern higher education, and they need the financial skills to effectively deploy the full range of financial resources embodied in revenue and expense flows, the statement of financial position, and cash flows. They should also be grounded in the possibilities and limitations associated with all forms of debt—for example, loans, bonds, leases, or leasebacks.

Principle Four: The chief marketing and academic officers should have the skills (professional and interpersonal) and experience to employ the resources generated by this paradigm to expand existing markets and to develop programs, products, and services for new markets.

Principle Five: The institution should produce five-year forecasts for the statement of activities, financial position, and cash flow that is shared and discussed in depth with the board of trustees. These forecasts should establish upper- and lower-sensitivity boundaries for major revenue flows to identify what could happen if unexpected events have an adverse impact on financial performance; the forecast should be integrated into the budget planning model. Annually, the president and chief administrative officers should revise the forecast model to account for missing factors and to keep it relevant to known or expected events for the next five years.

Principle Six: Cash needs to be sufficient to support operations and to cover debt payments (such as a ratio equal to 30 percent of expenses plus an amount needed to cover debt payments, when unexpected events occur).

Principle Seven: Middle administrative expenses (administration, staffing, and nonpersonnel expenses) should be cut significantly and should only be expanded to produce new revenue or to respond to large-scale growth.

Principle Eight: The president, CFO, and other senior administrative officers should establish metrics to develop and monitor the strategic financial plan. Performance metrics should cover basic financial drivers like enrollment, class size, and any factor that affects the scale and flow of revenue and expenses into, through, or from the institution. Metrics should also include standard measures of financial health – net asset ratio, cash ratio, net asset growth rates, and the Composite Financial Index.[6]

SUMMARY

The strategic-driven financial management paradigm is designed to change the way in which colleges and universities use and revise their current financial conditions. The specific intent of this paradigm is to improve operational performance, reduce expenses, employ assets to their highest use, create a strategic investment fund, respond to strategic opportunities, guide budget development, and monitor budgets so that performance conforms to specific performance metrics. Keep in mind that the board of trustees is a critical and necessary element of a strategic financial paradigm. Using this strategy toward accreditors, regulators, creditors, or other interested parties suggests that the institution does not understand the purpose of the paradigm, which is to produce financial viability and not hide or distort it.

The chapters "Economic Equilibrium," "Measuring Financial Health," "Forecast Modeling," and "Price and Discounts" will talk about specific

---

[6] The mechanics of the Composite Financial Index (CFI) can be found in R. E. Salluzzo, P. Tahey, F. J. Prager, & C. J. Cowen, *Ratio Analysis in Higher Education* (4th ed.), Washington DC: KPMG and Prager, McCarthy & Sealy, 1999. The most recent edition is available through the National Association of College and University Business Officers.

strategies to implement the paradigm. Here are several takeaway points that highlight the strategic-driven financial paradigm and several suggestions for readings to supplement understanding of the paradigm.

Takeaway Points

1. The college administration needs to appreciate the value embedded in the statement of financial position of their institutions.
2. Financial management is more than producing a positive net income. It must incorporate management of income flows through the statements of activities, financial position, and cash flow.
3. The president, CFO, and other chief administrative officers need to annually review the financial condition of the institution.
4. The college should have a five-year forecast model that shows how budgets and other financial decisions affect the financial statements and significant financial metrics of the college.

SUPPLEMENTAL READINGS

These readings may assist the senior administration during strategic planning sessions.

Townsley, Michael K. "Brinkmanship, Planning, Smoke, and Mirrors". *Planning for Higher Education* (summer) 19: 2, 1991: pp. 7–32.

Townsley, Michael K. "A Strategic Model for Enrollment-Driven Private Colleges." *Journal for Higher Education Management* (winter/summer) 8: 2, 1993; pp. 57-56.

Townsley, Michael K. "Deficit Prevention: Budget Control Model for Enrollment Dependent Colleges." *Business Officer* (October), National Association of College and University Business Officers, 1994; pp. 40–44.

Townsley, Michael K. *The Small College Guide to Financial Health (second edition)*. Washington, DC: National Association of College and University Business Officers, 2003.

Townsley, Michael K. "Leveraging facilities for competitive advantage; Essay 5." In Fennell, M. & Miller, S.D. (eds.), *Presidential Perspectives*, Philadelphia: Aramark, 2007; pp. 1-5.

Salluzzo, R. E., Tahey, P., Prager, F. J., and Cowen, C. J. *Ratio Analysis in Higher Education (fourth edition)* Washington, DC: KPMG and Prager, McCarthy & Sealy, 1999.

Townsley, Michael K. *Strategic Turnaround Toolbox*. Washington, DC: National Association of College and University Business Officers, 2007.

Townsley, Michael K. *Weathering Turbulent Times*. Washington, DC: National Association of Colleges and Business Officers, 2009.

CHAPTER 2

Economic Equilibrium

Economic equilibrium is a state of long-term financial sustainability for an institution of higher education. Richard Cyert, who developed the concept, set these conditions for a state of *economic equilibrium*:

1. There is sufficient quality and quantity of resources to fulfill the *mission* of an institution.
2. The organization maintains
   a   The purchasing power of its financial assets.
   b   Its facilities in satisfactory condition. [1]

Cyert's equilibrium is mission driven and is a fragile state that depends on income flows from operations and capital gifts to maintain the purchasing power of its financial assets and its facilities in satisfactory condition. Colleges need a dynamic state of economic equilibrium in which financial resources grow so as to avoid a state of disequilibrium. An institution cannot assume that positive but small changes in net income and financial assets are sufficient to either stave off disequilibrium or to sustain a state of economic equilibrium.

When an institution's financial condition has eroded to the point where it's cash and financial reserves have been seriously depleted, developing a strategic plan to achieve a dynamic state of equilibrium is difficult. Easy decisions, such as raising tuition or simply cutting expenses across the board, can be counterproductive if it pushes the college outside its competitive boundaries[7]. As Richard Cyert noted,

> "[T]he trick of managing the contracting organization is to break the vicious circle which tends to lead to disintegration of the organization. Management must develop counter forces which will allow the organization to maintain viability."[2]

In sum, boards of trustees must expect more from presidents and chief financial officers than a simple budget that only responds to current financial and economic conditions.

EQUILIBRIUM PRINCIPLES

Cyert's equilibrium can be restated as a set of principles:

- *Financial Equilibrium* is a financial state where a college has the financial resources (net assets) to sustain its mission and to provide for future generations of students.
- *Disequilibrium* is evident when a college has a history of: deficits, low or non-existent cash reserves, excess endowment draws, loans from the endowment, short-term cash loans, large deferred maintenance claims, and net assets shrinking or growing at a rate less than the rate of inflation.
- *Reaching a state of financial equilibrium* requires the elimination of the causes of disequilibrium.
- *The difference between equilibrium and disequilibrium* is the <u>equilibrium gap</u>.

---

[7] Competitive boundaries refer to a matrix with price and quality as axes of the matrix. A specific market is depicted as a smaller square within the matrix which includes potential students who prefer to enroll at a specific college with a particular level of price and quality.

DISEQUILIBRIUM

Disequilibrium is an erosion of the capital resources needed to support the mission of the institution while maintaining its purchasing power and its facilities in satisfactory condition. Capital resources comprise cash reserves, investments, plant, and the credit capacity of the institution. The following examples show how the internal economics of an institution can be put into a state of disequilibrium.

Cash flow disequilibrium often occurs during periods when operating deficits absorb cash reserves. Deficits can result from one of the following or a combination of these conditions: endowments decline in value and fail to generate increased flows to revenue, net tuition is uncompetitive; operational and capital costs are too high; gifts are inadequate; government initiatives increase costs or decrease revenue flows; and/or the demographics of student markets change in unexpected ways.

Investment disequilibrium happens when financial markets fall dramatically and may continue the fall over several fiscal years. This as noted with cash flow disequilibrium denies revenue and cash flows to operations.

Gross and net tuition disequilibrium commonly ensues when enrollment falls because of changes in demographics, fierce price competition, not keeping current with skills or academic programs sought by potential students, and rising attrition rates.

Cost disequilibrium from plant operations may result when a college produces insufficient net income to cover the cost of depreciation; unexpected costs of repairs outpace available net income; or operational costs of new or renovated buildings or equipment are higher than expected.

Cost disequilibrium from operations may arise from a variety of causes: new government regulations, necessity of adding student services to reduce attrition, inflation, and/or adding staff or faculty at mid-year without understanding the full costs when compensation for these positions are annualized. Cost disequilibrium is also found whenever the implications of adding new expenses are not taken into account. Cost disequilibrium can have a synergistic effect with revenue if a new revenue-producing program fails to generate targeted revenue, but the fixed costs of operating the program cannot be reduced.

Cost disequilibrium from capital projects may follow when construction costs from unfunded projects run higher than expected, variable interest loans or bond interest rates are higher than expected, or grant revenue for capital projects are less than pledged.

Credit capacity disequilibrium is a cumulative condition that is present when the financial condition of the institution deteriorates leading to requirements of higher interest rates. Also, lending agencies can impose covenants (conditions) that limit the financial discretion of an institution with low credit ratings. These covenants may prevent the institution from developing strategies to strengthen its financial condition if the college cannot take on addition debt or add programs that temporarily reduce net income.

STRATEGIES FOR ELIMINATING THE EQUILIBRIUM GAP

Here are several strategies that are common place in higher education for eliminating the Equilibrium Gap. The particular strategies selected will depend upon opportunities, both internally and externally; resources that it can use; and constraints on a particular strategic option.

1. *Enrollment, Recruitment, and Retention*
   a. Enrollment, recruitment, and retention strategies are attractive to most private colleges[8] because enrollment generates more than 60% of their revenue.[3,4] For most

---

[8] Seventy-five percent of private colleges fall into the tuition-dependent category.

public institutions, enrollment is the single factor that determines their financial condition.

b. The structure of the plan will depend upon the college's student market, competition, financial aid resources, academic offerings, and willingness of the board, faculty, and state and accrediting authorities to permit the institution to redesign, delete, or add new programs to the curriculum.

c. Admission strategies are complicated by the net cost to students, the student's long-term debt, the right mix of programs, and the pay-off when the student graduates and looks for employment (Graduate and professional schools add another level of complexity for student choice of a college and will not be considered here.) Admission campaigns today have to be aggressive with continuous follow-up until the prospective student is sitting in the classroom.

d. Retaining students once they are in college is an imperative given the cost of finding and admitting new students. Every student lost before finishing a full course of study forces the college to find a replacement. The result is that new student campaigns have to be devised to produce excess enrollment to offset attrition during the period that the cohort is enrolled. Most students, who do leave, will leave by the end of the first year. The evidence suggests that retention depends on how well the student did in high school. If a new student leaves high school in the upper two-thirds of her/his class, and her/his parents believe that a degree is essential for success in life, then the probability of graduating within six years is high.[5] If a student did not do well in high school and is the lower third of their high school graduating class, and college is merely a place to avoid earning a living, then persistence is low.[6]

2. *Gifts and Grants*

Gifts and grants play a critical role in most institutions even tuition-dependent colleges because these resources provide income to reach budgetary breakeven. Plans to solicit gifts and grants have to consider the cost inherent in seeking money from alumni, friends of the college, corporate grants, foundation grants, and government grants. A college at disequilibrium must allocate its resources (people, time, and money) only to efforts that have a high probability for a payoff in the short and medium term. Writing documents for foundation and government grants can quickly absorb the meager resources of a struggling college and often there is little chance for a payoff. Moreover, long-term gift or grant projects should be postponed until the college nears its point of equilibrium. For example, asking for major gifts requires a long-term campaign where the president or a senior staff member dedicates a large portion of her/his time to the care and feeding of wealthy donors or foundations. Fly-in and fly-out visits will not work; the president must care about the person and understand their needs, hopes, and intentions.

3. *Endowments*

Endowments, which are treated by many as the panacea for all financial problems, do not simply grow incrementally every year. Endowments are also another source of exasperation when endowments decline in value during major financial market crashes as happened from 2001 to 2002 and 2008 to 2009. When a struggling college invests a good portion of its time adding funds to the endowment, they must also recognize that falling financial markets have large and unanticipated effects on net income (statement of activities) and the balance sheet (statement of financial positions). When endowments lose market value, the investment loss could produce sizeable deficits. Deficits and reduction in the value of net assets may violate debt covenants and lower the score on the DOE test of financial responsibility, which could lead to government penalties.

Investment committees have conflicting preferences. They would probably prefer that the college maximize its returns to build investment value over the long term. Savvy investment committees see the problem of losses in financial markets as a short-term problem for the CFO, but they believe that their charge is to build the wealth of the college over the long term. However, the CFO must explain to the board and the investment committee the fiscal and financial implications from selecting high-risk/high-return investment strategies.

4. *Auxiliaries*

Too many colleges and universities overlook net revenues from auxiliary operations. It is dismaying to find colleges where residence halls, food services, or bookstores regularly yield deficits. At a minimum, auxiliaries should cover their direct expenses plus related interest expenses and principal payments for their debt. If the auxiliary cannot achieve this elementary financial goal, the CFO should devise a plan to align operational performance with this goal. Institutions at disequilibrium should outsource auxiliary operations that cannot support their own costs.

5. *Cost Controls*

Controlling costs is essential for institutions at disequilibrium. They may discover that generating revenue to close a growing equilibrium gap is neigh impossible. Several cost control solutions that are effective include: consortia, outsourcing services, cutting back on middle-level management, and rigorously cutting unjustified costs.

6. *New Initiatives*

Most equilibrium strategies include new initiatives, especially if they promise sufficient scale to speed up the closing of the equilibrium gap. Too often, presidents and chief administrative officers waste their scarce time tinkering around the edges on projects with either a small probability of success or a small chance of generating significant results. Before a new strategic initiative is selected, it should be tested against the institution's financial or budget planning model, and if it involves a new academic program, its success in the market should be tested. Here is a simple list of new initiatives:

1. Joint ventures, between community colleges and four-year institutions
2. Synergistic initiatives:
    a. Between colleges to provide courses and degrees that one or the other or both cannot do on their own
    b. With corporations to provide specific skill or management training that leads to a degree
    c. That form partnerships with professional organizations, colleges, or other entities so that students can earn professional certification that fits into a building block degree
    d. That establish a consortium with other colleges to offer on-line programs that reduce their costs of delivery and expand their markets.

3. Building block degree programs in which students can earn certificates, course credit, and transfer credit from other agencies and colleges (example, MOOC courses) that can be put together into degree credits
4. Re-engineering administrative processes by replacing offices with administrative networks
5. Refinancing debt to reduce interest expenses
6. Monitoring changes in the labor market with human resource managers to devise new academic programs for new skills required by the labor market.

Table 1

Equilibrium Gaps

Disequilibrium Sources	Amount
Net Tuition	
Operations	
Cash	
Capital	
Credit	
Total	

SUMMARY

Strategic economic equilibrium plans require constant and regular monitoring of key activities by the board of trustees and president. Monitoring should include monthly reports and benchmarks for admissions, retention, endowment performance, gifts, and new initiatives. Whether plans are working well and especially when they are not working well, key leaders must be ready to explain how a plan can be revised to reach a dynamic state of equilibrium. Equilibrium plans may require soul searching to determine if they can best serve their mission and, in particular, their students through a merger.[7]

Equilibrium is the boundary level for colleges and universities seeking to prosper. By reaching and maintaining equilibrium, the institution should be producing excess revenues that will permit the college to survive unexpected and financially-costly events and to grow to better serve its mission and its students.

TAKEAWAY POINTS

1. Economic Equilibrium is reached when an institution can fulfill its mission with adequate quantity and quality by maintaining the purchasing power of financial resources and maintaining facilities in satisfactory condition.

2. A primary financial goal for an institution of higher education should be to achieve a dynamic state of economic equilibrium (the strategies are not aimed at one point in the future but should incorporate means to keep pace with changes shaping the financial condition of the institution).

3. Equilibrium strategies follow from an equilibrium gap analysis that compares the actual financial state of the institution against a set of factors critical to achieving equilibrium.

4. Economic equilibrium outcomes must be continuously monitored and financial strategies revised to account for changes in the mission of the institution, student markets, academic programs, financial assumptions, and major changes in the economy or financial markets.

ENDNOTES

[1] Ruger, A., J. Canary, and S. Land (2006) "The President's Role in Financial Management" in <u>A Handbook for Seminary Presidents</u>; edited by G. Lewis and L.; William B. Erdman Publishing Company; Grand Rapids, Michigan.

[2] Cyert, R. (July, August 1978) *The Management of Universities of Constant or Decreasing Size*; <u>Public Administration Review</u>; p. 345.

[3] JMA Higher Ed Stats (2003); *Management ratios 2002 private colleges, universities, catalog #3690103.* Boulder, CO: John Minter and Associates.

[4] JMA Higher Ed Stats (2008) *Strategic higher education trends at a glance: F2 2002. csv and F2 2007.csv financial data.* Boulder, CO: John Minter and Associates.

[5] Zemsky, Robert and Penney Oedel (1983) <u>The Structure of College Choice</u>. College Entrance Examination Board: New York.

[6] Adelman, C. (2006) "The toolbox revisited: Paths to degree completion from high school to college" Washington, DC: U.S. Department of Education.

[7] Townsley, M. (2002); *The Small College Guide to Financial Health*. Washington, DC: NACUBO; p. 180

CHAPTER 3

Measuring Financial Health

Government agencies, banks, accreditors, credit analysts, and boards of trustees continually seek a way to estimate the current (and predict the future) financial viability of an institution of higher education. There are multiple reasons for wanting to know the financial condition, but the main reason is to determine whether the institution has the resources to accomplish its mission. Institutions of higher education present several challenges to analysts attempting to determine whether a particular financial measure can predict the long-term consequences of deteriorating financial health. Several challenges include the effect of government subsidies on student choice, the capacity of endowment investments to support operations, the impact of technology on operational costs and student demand, and the competitive rate of growth for tuition and fees. The central question, given the potential that the preceding challenges will undermine the financial capacity of some or even many private colleges and universities, is whether they have the resources to effectively compete for students. Students are the bread and butter for most private institutions; if the institutions lose their competitive edge, then their future may be compromised.

Four methodologies have emerged in the past several decades to measure financial health: a set of classic financial ratios from business that have been applied to higher education; a set of indicators utilized by credit agencies to measure credit risk; the composite financial index (CFI) used by many private audit firms to estimate the financial health of private institutions; and economic equilibrium analysis, which a major financial association for seminaries have recommended to their institutions. Over the years, a number of private colleges and universities have applied these methods to identify financial vulnerabilities facing their institutions and to formulate financial strategies to overcome financial crises. Several of these tools, in particular the CFI and equilibrium analysis, can provide key administrators with significant insight into the factors that could endanger their ability to remain competitive through this period of historic change. They can use these insights to build a financial strategy that strengthens institutional resources so that they can effectively respond to the emerging challenges that threaten their institution.

Further information about economic equilibrium analysis is available in the Appendix, and so it will not be examined further beyond the following comment. Economic equilibrium is a necessary condition of financial health because it gets at the essence of financial health: the preservation and enhancement of institutional resources to carry out the mission of the college. The economic equilibrium analysis should be a component of any report on financial health regardless of whether or not the other three tools—financial ratios, credit analytics, or CFI—are applied to the test of financial viability.

CLASSIC FINANCIAL RATIOS OF LIQUIDITY

There are three liquidity ratios (cash to operating expenses, current ratio, and uncollectible receivables ratios) that prove valuable to higher education as part of a standard rubric for measuring financial health. Most financial studies of businesses incorporate liquidity ratios because they measure whether sufficient funds are available that can be easily converted to cash to cover its current financial obligations. The same liquidity issues face higher education—that is, whether the institution can quickly convert short-term assets into cash to cover expenses, current liabilities, and current debt obligations. If a college is caught short on cash, it may be able to sidestep its inability to cover payables. However, if it is unable to keep current on the payroll, taxes, or current debt service, then the college could be in deep trouble. What follows is a brief outline of the purpose, structure, benchmarks, and data sources for each ratio.

1. Liquidity—Cash to Operating Expense Ratio:
   a. Purpose: To determine if the institution has sufficient cash to cover its planned operating expenses.
   b. Ratio Structure: Cash to operating expenses where cash is simply cash on hand; operating expenses are the budgeted expenses for the year.
   c. Benchmark: The cash ratio is presumed to be equivalent to a portion of the year in terms of months. A ratio of 8 percent is equivalent to cash for a month of expenses, whereas a 40 percent ratio is equivalent to five months of expenses. Usually this ratio should be greater than 25 percent to cover expenses during the summer when cash receipts are at their lowest ebb.
   d. Source of Data: This ratio is one of those cases where the denominator can either be budgeted expenses so that the college can estimate coverage for the coming year, or it can be audited operating expenses to estimate the trend for the cash ratio.

2. Liquidity—Current Ratio:
   a. Purpose: To estimate if there are sufficient current assets that can be converted to cash in the event of an emergency.
   b. Ratio Structure: Current assets to current liabilities where current assets typically include cash, receivables, inventory, short-term marketable securities, or any other asset that can be quickly converted to cash.
   c. Benchmark: This ratio should have a value greater than 1:1 because several of the current assets, such as receivables and inventory, may not be fully convertible into cash.
   d. Source of Data: Internal data and IRS 990 reports provide the necessary numbers.

3. Liquidity—Uncollectible Receivables Ratio:
   a. Purpose: To estimate the percentage of receivables that are uncollectible.
   b. Ratio Structure: Uncollectible receivables to total receivables where uncollectible receivables are those receivables that have been expensed as bad debt; total receivables are the total of outstanding receivables.
   c. Benchmark: As the uncollectible receivable ratio approaches 12 percent, it reaches a point where approximately a month's worth of receivables cannot be collected. The institution should watch the trend in this ratio to see if it is increasing over time. It is recommended that the ratio should be computed each month.
   d. Sources for Data: Internal data and IRS 990 reports provide the necessary numbers.

The preceding financial ratios do not provide a single value that designates financial health, but when taken cumulatively, they offer a rough picture of the financial condition of an institution. For instance, if liquidity (cash, current ratio, uncollectible receivables) is weak and becoming weaker over time, then there is an increasing risk that the institution cannot continue to deliver on its mission.

CREDIT RISK FACTORS FOR MEASURING FINANCIAL HEALTH

Credit agencies rate the credit risk of institutions of education that are planning to sell bonds directly or through a state agency on the open market. They also continue to rate the risk of those institutions that have used their institution for an earlier rating. The purpose of credit rating is to determine whether an institution has and will continue to have the resources to make interest and principal payments. Most of the credit rating factors for higher education were originally derived from the credit ratings for businesses and governmental agencies. These ratings are closely watched by bond investors, governmental oversight agencies, and some regional accreditation commissions. Even though many private colleges do not sell bonds and use financial institutions for their debt requirements, the basic credit factors of the large credit agencies are often used by these financial institutions to validate whether a college is credit worthy.

The credit analysis factors described here are characteristic of the factors used by major credit rating agencies. In this instance, the ratios are from Moody's Investors Service,[a] which Moody's has subsequently revised since the original publication in 2001. The Moody's ratios include several nonfinancial measures such as matriculation and selectivity. These nonfinancial ratios get at whether a college has a deep student pool or must take whoever appears at the admissions office. In the first case, the college has greater pricing power, and in the second case the college is a price taker—that is, it can only charge what the market will bear.

Moody's ratios are a fruitful approach for private institutions that would like to estimate financial condition because the ratios can be benchmarked to Moody's regularly published medians and credit ratings for colleges and universities. In addition, these credit rating ratios will give an institution some insight into the issues which lenders could raise when it seeks to obtain a sizeable loan.

Nonfinancial Ratios: Selectivity and Matriculation (source of data: internal data resources reported by the admissions office)

1. Purpose: To estimate the depth of student demand for the institution.
2. Ratio Structure:
    a. *Selectivity Ratio*: The number of acceptances divided by the number of applications.
    b. *Matriculation Ratio*: The number admitted divided by the number of acceptances.

---

[a] See "Appendix II: Moody's Private College and University Ratio Definitions," *Moody's Investors Service: Private Colleges and Universities Outlook 2001/02 and Medians,* July, 2001.

c. As these two ratios increase, the market demand for the institution decreases and pricing becomes more problematic.

3. Benchmarks: Moody's Investor Service medians, or else medians from a competitive set drawn from IPEDS[10] or data compilation services such as John Minter & Associates.

***Financial Measures* used by Moody's Investor Services:** These are standard ratios used by Moody's to assess credit risk. It would be prudent for an institution preparing for a credit rating or having its credit rating reevaluated to determine how its finances compare to Moody's measures. Although other rating companies may use different ratios, these ratios tend to be typical for higher education.

1. Operational Ratios:
   a. *Operating Margin*:
      i. Purpose: To determine if the institution is generating sufficient net income to cover operating expenses.
      ii. Structure of Annual Operating Margin: Operating net after limiting investment income to 4.5 percent of the previous year's cash and investments, and deducting net assets released for construction divided by operating revenue given the 4.5 percent restriction and the deduction for net assets. (Determine whether there are sufficient operating revenues relative to operating expenses.)

   b. *Actual Debt Service Coverage*:
      i. Purpose: To estimate the amount of funds available to cover payment of debt service.
      ii. Structure of Actual Debt Service Coverage: Annual operational net, including interest and depreciation divided by actual principal and interest. (The trend in this ratio will show if there is a risk of losing the buffer that covers debt service expenses.)

---

10 Integrated Postsecondary Education System

   c. *Return on Financial Resources:*
- i. Purpose: To indicate if the institution has increased its financial resources exclusive of the plant.
- ii. Structure of Return on Financial Resources: The change in total financial resources (net asset minus net investment in plant) divided by the average total resources at the beginning and end of the year.

   d. *Benchmark Sources:*
- i. Moody's Investor Service medians.
- ii. Medians from a competitive set drawn from IPEDS.
- iii. Data from a compilation service such as John Minter & Associates.

2. Statement of Financial Position Ratios

   a. *Free Expendable Financial Resources to Operations:*
- i. Purpose: To identify the coverage of operating expenses by expendable financial resources.
- ii. Structure of Free Expendable Financial Resources to Operations: (Unrestricted and temporarily restricted net assets minus net investment in plant minus debt) divided by total operating expenses.
- iii. Benchmarks: Moody's Investor Service medians, or else medians from a competitive set drawn from IPEDS or a summary services such as John Minter & Associates.

   b. *Total Financial Resources per Student:*
- i. Purpose: To be used as a marker for comparison to medians for a competitive set or for a category of bond issuers.
- ii. Structure of the Total Financial Resources per Student: (Total net assets minus net investment in plant) divided by full-time students.
- iii. Benchmarks: Moody's Investor Service medians, or else medians from a competitive set drawn from

IPEDS or a data compilation service such as John Minter & Associates.

Moody's considers the selectivity ratio, free expendable resources to operations ratio, and the total financial resources per student ratio as critical factors in measuring the financial capacity of an institution to reliably cover its debt payments. By implication, these factors are also indicative of financial health.

COMPOSITE FINANCIAL INDEX (CFI)

The CFI is a rating system that evolved from a US Department of Education project designed to determine the eligibility of colleges to receive student aid funds. The index employs a set of "core ratios… represent[ing] key components in relation to financial risks that must be monitored consistently [by a college]."[1] The core ratios measure: the adequacy of funds for emergencies, short-term performance, changes in wealth, and the capacity to support long-term debt (the respective ratios are: the primary ratio, the net income ration, the return on assets ratio, and the viability ratio). The components of the core ratios are in Table 2.

Table 2

Composite Financial Index Ratios[2]

Primary Ratio	Total expendable net assets divided by total operating expenses
Net Income Ratio	Operating surplus or deficit divided by operating income
Return on Assets	Change in net assets divided by net assets at the beginning of the year
Viability Ratio	Total expendable net assets divided by total long-term debt.

Primary reserve ratio: This ratio measures the financial strength of an institution, indicating the surplus resources an institution could use for debt without recourse to additional net income (net asset) support from operations.[3] Preferably, the ratio increases at the same rate as growth in expenses.[4] If the primary ratio grows at a slower rate than expenses, then expendable net assets will represent a shrinking margin of protection during adversity.[5] A ratio of 0.4, a minimal standard, indicates sufficient capacity for short-term cash needs for 5 months (40 percent of 12 months).[6] Primary reserve values less than 0.15 suggest that the institution probably needs short-term loans to pay its bills and probably struggles to reinvest in its plant.[7]

Net income ratio: The scale and sign of the ratio suggest that operations are or are not contributing sufficiently to build reserves, cash flow, and cover debt payments. The outcome of the net income ratio also has a direct bearing on the other three CFI ratios: primary reserve, return on net assets, and viability.[8] According to Salluzzo, Tahey, and Prager, given the impact of depreciation, the net income ratio should fall in the 2-4 percent range.[9] Large deficits over a period of years are a "warning signal that management and the governing board should focus on restructuring the institution's income and expense streams."[10] A deficit in any one year is not cause for alarm "if the institution is financially strong, is aware of the causes…, and has…a plan to…cure the deficit."[11] There are two computational forms of this ratio.

Return on net assets ratio: The trend for this ratio indicates whether wealth is increasing or decreasing.[12] The CFI authors believe that given the volatility of the underlying asset returns (e.g., endowment funds), the *real* (discounted for inflation) value for the ratio should fall within the range of 3–4 percent.[13] The degree of volatility in the underlying assets depends on the mix of endowment-to-plant assets. The return on net assets ratio may be calculated by permanently removing restricted net assets from the numerator and denominator, leaving assets that are under the direct control of the institution and that can be redeployed for increasing revenue or decreasing expenses.[14] When liquid assets are turned into plant assets, the presumption is that the institution is adding to its productive capacity. Whether that assumption is true depends on the actual decision made and the uses of the funds.

Viability ratio: This ratio is "one of the most basic determinants of financial health because it measures if the institution can meet its debt obligations as of the balance sheet date."[15] The visibility ratio represents an institution's safety net in the event of extraordinarily adverse conditions. According to the experience of the CFI authors, the preferable range for this ratio is between "1.25 and 2.00."[16] When the ratio falls below 1:1 (expendable net assets match long-term debt), external agencies may see the institution as a credit risk and deny the institution access to capital.[17] Institutions may survive for long periods with a high level of debt leverage; but they lose their flexibility to raise capital, putting severe pressure on their current assets forcing business officers to borrow for short-term cash needs.[18]

The computation of the CFI score follows a four-step process. (Appendix 2 provides the algorithms and a template to compute the CFI) The reader should check with the latest version of <u>Ratio Analysis in Higher Education</u> for the newest edition of the CFI computation. The four step process involves:

1. Comte the value of each core ratio.
2. Convert ratio to a strength factor.
3. The strength factor is then weighted for the relative of that importance to the final CFI score. The CFI is a sum of the weighted strength values of the four core ratios.
4. The CFI Index is then assigned to one of ten levels of progressively stronger financial condition (see the scoring structure in Table 3).
5. Note: The CFI Index can then be assigned to one of ten levels of progressively stronger financial conditions (see the scoring table next).

Table 3

Consolidated Financial Index Scoring Scale[19]

Scale Level	CFI Scoring Range	Action
One	-1 to 1	Assess viability to survive.
Two	0 to 2	Reengineer the institution.
Three	1 to 3	
Four	2 to 4	Direct resources toward transformation.
Five	3 to 5	
Six	4 to 6	Focus resources to compete in future state.
Seven	5 to 7	
Eight	6 to 8	Experiment with new initiatives.
Nine	7 to 9	Achieve a robust mission with new initiatives.
Ten	> 9	Deploy resources to achieve a robust mission.

SUMMARY OF PERFORMANCE BOUNDARIES FOR CFI RATIOS

There are several general observations that are evident from the computation and the scoring table. A low CFI score of three or less indicates a high level of financial distress; a CFI greater than six indicates a financially strong and flexible college. A low CFI score suggests that an institution lacks the financial resources to effectively respond to the technological, economic, and regulatory challenges facing higher education. On the other hand, a high CFI score implies that an institution has adequate resources to respond to those challenges.

As the CFI scoring table illustrates, the scoring system is not a precise instrument; rather, it is indicative of action that an institution could make subject to the understanding of its particular case. As a result, a CFI score will fall within a range of possible actions. A particular CFI score can also be used to decode strategic and operational actions that the institution should take to improve or to strengthen its financial health. For example, a CFI score of 3.17 could be deconstructed into its four ratios, such that a specific CFI score of 3.17 might be due to a primary reserve value equaling 1.3, a net income value of 5 percent, a return on net assets value of 6 percent, and a viability ratio of 0.20. The institution could then target a strategic and operational plan to reinvigorate the components of the primary and viability ratios. How effective an institution is at improving its financial health will depend on the wit and wisdom of its leadership.

FINANCIAL METRICS

The preceding discussion of financial health is the basis for using financial metrics to manage financial health. Why do colleges and universities care about metrics? The answer is simple: government agencies, banks, and accreditors control access to resources and the authority to operate; and they increase the pressure on colleges to conform to new regulations and financial conditions. The consequences to a college that fails to measure up to third-party metrics can be devastating and may range from the loss of federal financial aid funds to the calling of a loan by a financial agency or the burden of paying for a costly line-of-credit. Because financial metrics can have adverse and consequential effects on the authority of the college to continue unfettered operations, the metric will act as a powerful incentive for colleges to design strategies and operational plans that target the factors built into the metrics. This outcome is not to be unexpected; it is how businesscs have operated because their performances are judged by third parties using commonly accepted metrics.

Metrics are a useful financial tool that institutions can use to get a clearer picture of their performance relative to external benchmarks and to regulatory and legal conditions set by external agencies. However, the challenge for colleges is how to design a financial strategy to achieve specific metric standards in a dual authority structure of shared governance that is often disruptive, especially when there is financial disarray.

A financial metric specifies the expected performance for a particular financial factor or relationship for several financial factors within an organization. A metric typically incorporates two components: the method of measuring the metric and a standard or benchmark for the metric. Metrics may be a ratio of two factors, be a rate of growth, or specify a single factor.[20] Examples of several financial metrics employed in higher education are: the ratio of net income to total revenue, the rate of growth for total revenue, and the value of cash reserves.

Benchmarks set out a required performance standard for the metric, with standards being set by: government regulations, commonly-accepted practices, or agreed-upon covenants in a debt instrument. Examples of metrics include the Department of Education's financial responsibility test, the Composite Financial Index (CFI), and cash reserve requirements in a bond instrument.

The purpose of a metric is to signify whether performance is better than, less than, or equal to a benchmark. When performance is subpar, the president should revise strategies and plans to achieve the expected performance standard. When leaders choose a metric to measure financial performance, they also accept by implied condition that their financial decisions must yield results that conform to the performance levels delineated by the metric.

Metrics need to be accompanied by a reporting system that regularly compares actual performance with the metric benchmark. The reporting system should follow trends for the set of metrics used by the institution to determine whether changes are favorable or unfavorable.

Given that metrics are only as effective as a reporting system, the following processes are suggested to complement the metric reporting system.

1. The president and chief administrative officers must formally meet, review performance, and determine if and where changes need to be made. Their findings should be clearly stated in a formal document describing the financial state of the college and any strategic or operational changes that are needed to achieve the performance level required by the metrics.
2. The president must present the metric performance report to the board of trustees so that they can evaluate if the plans fit the mission and strategy of the institution.

The negative side of metrics is that they may limit reasonable options, particularly at a financially-weakened institution. For instance, during the transition from a weak to a viable financial state, a college may have to extend the period when deficits are reported because it spends more money to rebuild its market share. This college needs to reallocate its resources and invest in new programs. Financial metrics will become necessary conditions imposed by third parties to assess whether an institution has the financial resources to support its financial obligations and to sustain its mission.

FINAL NOTE ON MEASURING FINANCIAL HEALTH

An institution does not guarantee itself that it truly understands its financial condition by using financial ratios, credit rating ratios, or the CFI. There is more to the picture of financial health than financial numbers, as suggested by Moody's nonfinancial ratios. An analysis of financial health as a prelude to strategic planning requires that an institution build a case that looks not only at financial variables but also at factors that drive those variables. Before institutional leaders design a strategic plan, they understand their current state. Once, institutional leaders have reached consensus on findings and the condition of the institution, they should convert their discussions and findings into a case study. The following are several factors that are typically part of a case study of financial health: a historic narrative of the past decade which includes description of its markets, tuition discounts; enrollments; graduation rates, fixed costs of operations, variable expenses, deferred capital expenses; new and current capital expenses; government regulations; accrediting commission comments; currency of technology; and any changes in instructional delivery systems.

Summary

Metrics provide measures measures for evaluating the financial condition of an institution. The purpose of the several metrics cited here is to determine the financial health of the institution benchmarked to established, for example, the Composite Financial Index, credit agency standards, or institutional goals. Metrics are part of regular assessments of performance and strategic plans. During strategic reviews, operational plans should be revised as necessary so that performance will achieve the standard established for any metric that fell below expectations.

Takeaway Points

1. Management must identify a methodology to assess if strategic goals are being achieved.
2. Assessing financial health should take place annually.
3. Deviations in financial condition goals (benchmarks) need to become part of strategic and operational plan reviews.
4. The budget should be developed in reference to the findings of the annual financial health assessment.

ENDNOTES

1   R. E. Salluzzo, P. Tahey, F. J. Prager, and C. J. Cowen, *Ratio Analysis in Higher Education, fourth edition* (KPMG and Prager, McCarthy & Sealy, 1999): p. 10.

2   See R. E. Salluzzo, et al., p. 11, 14–15, 20.

3   See R. E. Salluzzo et al., p. 11.

4   See R. E. Salluzzo, et al., p. 11.

5   See R. E. Salluzzo, et al., p. 11.

6   See R. E. Salluzzo, et al., p. 14.

7   See R. E. Salluzzo, et al., p. 14.

8   See R. E. Salluzzo, et al., p. 14.

9   See R. E. Salluzzo et al., p. 15.

10 See R. E. Salluzzo, et al., p. 15.

11 See R. E. Salluzzo, et al., p. 14.

12 See R. E. Salluzzo, et al., p. 17

13 See R. E. Salluzzo, et al., p. 17.

14 See R. E. Salluzzo, et al., p. 20.

15 See R. E. Salluzzo, et al., p. 21.

16 See R. E. Salluzzo, et al., p. 22.

17 See R. E. Salluzzo, et al., p. 22.

18 See R. E. Salluzzo, et al., p. 22.

19 See R. E. Salluzzo, et al., p. 24.

20 Martin Cave, Stephen Hanney, Maurice Kogan, and Gillian Trevet, *The Use of Performance Indicators in Higher Education* (London: Jessica Kingsley Publishers, 1988): pp. 17–18.

Chapter 4

Forecast Modeling

The effectiveness of strategic plans, operational budgets, and capital budgets are pure guesswork without a comprehensive financial forecasting model that tests assumptions, strategies, and operational plans, and that changes in the way in which the institution employs its financial resources. This section will examine the purpose, structure, and major components of financial model that can be of considerable use to chief financial officers.

Forecast Model Purposes

The main purposes of forecast models are to: estimate operational income, and test alternative strategic options. Other valuable uses for forecasts include testing changes in regulations, higher education markets, and financial markets. Although these changes may be beyond the control of an institution, they can have profound effects on its financial condition.

Forecast Model Conditions:

There are two imperatives to the design of an effective budget model: the model should be valid (represent budgetary operations) and reliable (consistently predict outcomes). In order to be valid and reliable, the model should reflect the budgetary operations of the institution by including operational revenues and expenses, capital projects, debt service, and the financial dynamics that drive the budget. In order to accomplish the validity and reliability imperatives, the models should be built in response to these further conditions:

1. The forecast design should use a base period of three years with data drawn from audited financial and operational performance.
2. Enrollment, class sections, or any other operational data must be reconciled to the audited budgetary data.
3. The forecast should incorporate variables that drive changes in revenue and expenses.
4. Revenue and expenses may also change through additions or deletions to revenue, expenses, debt, or assets that over the period of the forecast may then be affected by the factors that drive changes in revenue and expenses.
5. Variability rates should be included in forecasts in order to express a relationship between enrollment and expenses (such as new positions, additional space, or other costs that vary with the number of students).
6. As each year is added to a forecast, predictability and reliability decline. Forecasts will vary through decisions made within the institution and through forces external to the institution during planning and during the forecast period. Multiple year forecasts need to be updated annually.
7. Internal decisions explicitly affect a forecast when they are stated in board actions, presidential decisions, budget plans, and implicitly when unplanned actions of the administration, staff, or faculty drive changes in revenue or expenses. Again, forecasts need updating annually.
8. External changes may be classified as known knowns (e.g., changes in laws that affect student aid), known unknowns (e.g., changes in regulations that might come from reauthorization of the Higher Education Act), and unknown unknowns (e.g., unpredictable financial market crashes or the appearance of new technology).

9. Forecasts can also be shaped by the ability of internal managers to carry out the plans. Rates of change for forecasts are limited by how quickly large increases can take effect given current institutional capacity, markets, financial structure, the skills of the employees, and their time and cost.

10. Reductions in expenses are limited by legal constraints, contracts, opposition, and other actions that retard the termination of a program, facility, or set of employees.

11. The precision of the forecast model depends upon the clarity of the data available to the model.

12. In most cases, the forecast is prepared by the chief financial officer in consultation with other budgeting officers.

FORECAST MODEL COMPONENTS

For a forecast model to meet the validity and reliability criteria stated above, it must encompass all components and factors that will drive the operation of the college during the period covered by the forecast. Typically, a sophisticated forecast model will include the following components: variables, enrollments, fixed cost changes, new revenue or expense departments, capital projects, debt service, net income, and financial metric tests. These components are described below.

1. *Variable Component:* Variable factors can be changed by increasing or decreasing the factor for each year of the forecast. Examples of variable factors include changes in: tuition rates, tuition discount rates, pay rates, benefits, utilities, bad debt percentages, and inflation rates.

Table 4

Sample Variables Table

Factor	Fiscal Year #1	Fiscal Year #2	Fiscal Year #3	Fiscal Year #4	Fiscal Year #5
Tuition					
Faculty Pay					
Medical Insurance					

2. *Enrollment Forecast Component:* The enrollment component arrays student flows based upon either fixed estimates or rates of changes for new students, attrition rates for continuing students, and graduation rates. The component should be disaggregated by price so that enrollments with different pricing levels are modeled independently. Examples of disaggregated enrollments are undergraduate, masters, and doctoral degrees and/or day, evening, and online programs.

Table 5

Sample Undergraduate Enrollment Forecast

Factor	Rates	Fiscal Year #1	Fiscal Year #2	Fiscal Year #3	Fiscal Year #4	Fiscal Year #5
First-Year Students						
Undergraduate Continuing Students						
Graduate Students						
Attrition						
Graduation						
Total Enrollment						

3. *Changes in Fixed Costs Component:* These changes could include additions or deletions to faculty, staff, administration, plant, or IT.

Table 6

Sample Fixed Cost Changes Table

Factor	Fiscal Year #1	Fiscal Year #2	Fiscal Year #3	Fiscal Year #4	Fiscal Year #5
Count of Full-Time Faculty					
Pay Rate					
Total Cost					

4. *New Revenue or Expense Components:* Whenever a new revenue or expense department is added, it should have its own forecast component with the necessary factors that drive changes in revenue or expenses. The data is then fed into the appropriate revenue or expense section, or it can be fed into a separate section as new programs. Revenue and expense departments would be set up in the same manner as the sample table but without the revenue section.

Table 7

Sample New Tuition Revenue / Expense Department

Factor	Fiscal Year #1	Fiscal Year #2	Fiscal Year #3	Fiscal Year #4	Fiscal Year #5
Enrollment					
Tuition Rate					
Tuition Revenue					
Full-Time Faculty	Refer to Sample Fixed Cost Table for Expensing Costs				

Staff	Refer to Sample Fixed Cost Table for Expensing Costs
Administration	Refer to Sample Fixed Cost Table for Expensing Costs.
Benefits	
Taxes	
Supplies & IT	
IT	
Other Expenses	
Total Expenses	
Net	

5. *Capital Project Component:* The component should include all capital projects planned for each year of the forecast period. It should estimate the total cost of the project, method of funding, and depreciation. Depreciation should be fed back to operating expenses. In addition, if gifts are needed to fund the project, they should be entered in the gift section of the revenue budget. Debt should be estimated in the debt component.

Table 8

Sample Capital Project Table

Factor	Fiscal Year #1	Fiscal Year #2	Fiscal Year #3	Fiscal Year #4	Fiscal Year #5
Project Name					
Project Cost					
Depreciation					
Amount Funded by Debt					
Amount Funded by Gifts/Grants					
Amount Funded by Other Sources					

6. *Debt Service Component:* Any project to be funded by debt should include an amortization schedule with interest being posted to operating expenses and principal payments posted to nonoperating expenses.

Table 9

Sample Debt Service Component

	Fiscal Year #1	Fiscal Year #2	Fiscal Year #3	Fiscal Year #4	Fiscal Year #5
Project Name					
Total Principal	Place the amount in the correct year and figure interest and principle from that year.				
Interest Payment by Year					
Principle Payment by Year					

7. *Revenue, Expense, and Change in Net Assets Component:* Table 12 brings together the components to produce a net income.

8. *Financial Metrics Component:* The chief financial officer could add several financial metric components to the Operating Income Forecast. This component could include various financial metrics that should be checked, such as: the net tuition discount ratio, the CFI, and the Department of Education's (DOE) test of financial responsibility (this test can be found on the DOE site). The purpose of this component would be to determine if the financial condition of the institution is or is not being strengthened, and to check whether or not operational plans are achieving a state of equilibrium.

9. *Variability Rates*: the variability relationships between enrollment and expense factors depend upon institutional experience and are derived from iterative testing of the relationship.
10. *Forecast Stack*: The following table shows the forecast after all the components are stacked.

Table 10

Forecast Stack—Operating Income Statement

		Forecast Period				
	Three Years as Base	Fiscal Year #1	Fiscal Year #2	Fiscal Year #3	Fiscal Year #4	Fiscal Year #5
Enrollment						
Variable Factors						
Fixed Cost Factors						
Income Statement						
Revenue	List all revenue sources across the adjacent columns					
Expenses	List current expense centers, new expense departments, and interest and depreciation expenses from new capital projects.					
Net Income						

Table 11

Forecast Stack—Capital Projects and Financial Metrics

	Three Years as Base	Fiscal Year #1	Fiscal Year #2	Fiscal Year #3	Fiscal Year #4	Fiscal Year #5
Project						
Project Cost						
Funds from Debt						
Funds from Assets						
Funds from Operations						
Gift Funding						
Amount Internally Funded						
Depreciation						
Financial Metrics	List all metrics such as the CFI, DOE, and other financial metrics.					

When the work of computing the forecast is completed, there are several additional steps in order to prepare it as a report to the board of trustees, the president, and chief administrative officers. The first step is to have the computations vetted by another staff member of the finance area, or by the auditor, to provide assurance to recipients of the report of its validity and computational accuracy. The second step is to write a summary of the assumptions (changes in variables), new departments, and capital projects that drive the forecast. The next step is to convert the forecast summary into an income statement (statement of financial activities and identification of the financial metric) to be used as benchmarks. The last step is to list the contingencies and obstacles that would have to be considered in putting the forecast into operation. The forecast should be an integral part of the budget to show the short-term (one year) and long-term (five year) effects of an annual budget. It should also be employed as a tool in testing financial strategies.

Designing and running a financial forecast model will absorb a considerable effort on the part of the staff the first time that they build the model, and subsequently when they make major changes in financial strategies. It is wise for management to arrange for outside assistance to help build, to test, and to be available for problem solving with the model as computations are made with it.

Once a particular run of the forecast is accepted as the basis for operational and strategic planning, the forecast parameters should be updated annually based on actual experience and tested with financial plans or strategies.

SUMMARY

The purpose of a forecast is to test the effect of budgets, strategies and operational plans on the financial condition of the institution. The forecast should be sufficiently robust so that plans that include new operating departments (revenue generating and expense departments), capital projects, and new debt can be tested. In addition, the forecast should be able to test changes in a large number of revenue and expense drivers, such as enrollment, tuition and fees, tuition discounts, and compensation. Moreover, the forecast needs to estimate cash flows and the impact of budgets and strategies on net assets. Forecasts should also test competitive pricing and marketing strategies. The forecast should look forward at least five years with the results of the forecast presented to the chief administrative team in charge of budgets and strategic planning.

TAKEAWAY POINTS

1. The forecast model should be built upon the most recent audit of the statement of activities, statement of financial position, and cash flow report.
2. The model should include:
   a. Data from the current budget, strategic plans, and data on actual financial performance
   b. Modules for new programs, capital projects, and debt
   c. Variables, such as enrollment, etc, that can be tested to identify the optimum performance level.
3. The forecast should test budget assumptions, strategic options, and financing plans for capital projects.

CHAPTER 5

Price and Discounts

Setting tuition is changing dramatically under the pressure of threatened government regulations and vigorous competition from competitors. The old model of price as a proxy for quality and net price as a chance to give attractive candidates large scholarships (a source of braggadocio for parents about their children) is fading into the past. Evidence is mounting (as reported in the _Wall Street Journal_) that more schools are doing away with high sticker prices and setting tuition prices closer to their old net price. The problem is that price cutting has the potential to wipe out revenue if the old, higher education assumption that students are price inelastic[11] still applies. However, the results of price cutting at several private colleges suggest that students are becoming more price elastic.[12] It used to be that only a small segment of the student market (mainly working adult students) was price elastic; and even they became price inelastic as they passed from new students into first-, second-, third-, and fourth-year students.

Over the last several years, it appears that students and parents are becoming more elastic in their choices. According to news print, such as _The Chronicle of Higher Education_ and other professional associations, changes in student (parent) pricing behavior is due to declining discretionary income, loss of savings, underwater mortgages, and flat or declining government (state support primarily) financial

---

[11] Price inelasticity means that a drop in price does not produce a sufficient increase in volume to make up the loss in revenue.

[12] Price elastic means that as price is reduced, the volume increases to the extent that it generates more revenue; this is the old gasoline price wars concept.

aid. The result is that the days where headlines said that college tuition is growing faster than inflation will be replaced with news about an ever-growing number of colleges that are making sharp cuts in their sticker prices. Data from the College Board suggests that net tuition has been flat for the ten years, from 2003–04 to 2012–13.[1] Flat growth for net tuition suggests that colleges have increased discounts in the face of smaller student markets. Forecasts by the National Center for Education Statistics indicate that student markets will shrink further as birthrates have declined over the last several decades which will lead to fewer high school graduates. Moreover, the pool of potential new college students is smaller because families cannot afford the cost of a degree.

If the trends in pricing over the past several years turn out to be indicative of long-term trends in higher education, price competition will get very nasty. Private colleges and universities, especially small and medium institutions with small endowments, will find that managing price and the factors that drive price will become more important in their budgets and during strategic planning.

Markets and Pricing

As mentioned earlier, the ruling assumption about prices is that students are price (tuition price) inelastic. This assumption may no longer be true because circumstances have changed the economics behind students being price inelastic. Price inelasticity arises when purchasers do not have substitutes readily available that offer comparable qualities and lower prices. Over the past several decades, the factors governing the substitution of one institution for another has changed due to more flexible rules on transfer credits, returning adult students, online courses, and changes in governmental financial aid rules. As students have sought flexibility in transferring credits, they have moved to colleges that aggressively pursue them. As a result, colleges have had to increase tuition discounts and reduce their net prices, which has severely diminished their ability to avoid deficits.

The other problem haunting private colleges and universities is that a combination of the problem of price competition will only get worse as segments of the student market continue to decline, as predicted by the US Department of Education several years ago. In addition, the lingering effects of the Great Recession of 2007 and 2008 have diminished discretionary income normally used by families and students to fund the balance owed for tuition and fees after the tuition discount is deducted. Prospective students are moving down the tuition price scale because they lack the funds to pay for a more costly and maybe more prestigious school (i.e., the conundrum of higher tuitions equaling better quality).

The chickens may be coming home to roost as ever-rising prices drive students toward lower prices. For instance, *The Chronicle of Higher Education* reported that 50 percent of the colleges that they surveyed failed to achieve their enrollment goals for the fall of 2013.[2] If private colleges are unable to set a market rate price, their chance of attracting sufficient students to fill classrooms will quickly contract to the point where their financial viability fades away.

GOVERNMENT REGULATIONS

There are a variety of sources that could affect tuition and enrollments. For example, the Department of Education is proposing new regulations to govern the allocation of federal financial aid awards. As proposed by the DOE, financial aid will be distributed based on a double whammy of graduation rates and the employment of graduates. The employment rule will require colleges to track their graduates over the first several years of employment and report on their income. The DOE's rules will reduce financial aid to colleges with low graduation rates or with graduates who do not earn sufficient income to pay back their loans. If these rules come into effect, many colleges will find that they have to offset lost financial aid from the DOE with aid from internal sources. For institutions with small endowments and low enrollment growth, finding internal sources of financial aid will either be impossible or result in massive cuts to their programs. In addition, the competition for students could become virulent as institutions aggressively recruit new students by slashing their net tuition. Under these circumstances, pricing strategies will become the end all and be all of private institutions. As suggested in the preceding section, even without government reductions in financial aid, private colleges face huge problems in setting a tuition rate that reasonably covers costs and continues to draw prospective students.

THE EFFECT OF DEEP DISCOUNTING

Deep discounting of tuition potentially violates the basic rule that revenue lost to the price discount must be regained by larger enrollments. Even as students become more price elastic, it may not be large enough to attract enough students to offset lost revenue.

Table 12 illustrates what happens when the tuition discount rate keeps increasing: net tuition revenue declines as the tuition discount rate increases. The marginal rate of change nearly doubles when the discount rate increases from 35 percent to 45 percent and net tuition revenue declines for each rate. Of course, this table does not take into account the inelasticity of tuition prices where increases in price do not necessarily lead to commensurate losses in tuition revenue. Colleges will need to carefully analyze the effect when they increase the tuition discount rate so that they avoid the unintended result of tuition revenue dropping off precipitously and unexpectedly, and they lose cash flow to pay for operational expenses. The analysis will require them to survey what is generally happening with discounts, and they will need to conduct a statistical analysis to estimate the price elasticity of their students and of their student pool.

Table 12

Impact of Different Tuition Discount
Rates on Net Tuition Revenue

	2005	2006	2007	2008
Posted Tuition	$27,000	$27,000	$27,000	$27,000
Financial Aid Discount Rate	25%	30%	40%	50%
Net Tuition	$20,250	$18,900	$17,550	$14,850
Enrollment (8% rate of increase)	1,500	1,620	1,750	1,890
Net Tuition Revenue	$30,375,000	$30,618,0000	$28,343,520	$25,509,168
Marginal Change		-$243,000	-$2,274,480	-$2,834,352
Marginal Rate of Change		1%	-7%	-10%

PRICE ALGORITHM

The basic pricing formula in most private institutions is:

> Price = (Total Expenses minus Nontuition Revenue)/
> (Enrollment plus Tuition Discounts).

The key factors that determine price in this formula are expenses, the scale of nontuition revenue (gifts, grants, endowment income, etc.), tuition discounts, and enrollment. Expenses can be disaggregated by the factors that make up the expenses of the institution, such as payroll, supplies, equipment, plant, depreciation, or interest. The chief pricing issue for all but the most heavily-endowed colleges is how to set a price that does not deter students from enrolling and also provides sufficient revenue with nontuition revenue to cover budgetary expenses. It necessarily follows that net tuition is of corollary importance because not only must the net price produce sufficient income with nontuition revenue to balance expenses, but it must also generate sufficient cash with nontuition cash to pay its bills. This chapter will lay out several ways in which gross or sticker tuition price and net price is established, and how regulatory limits on tuition might shape pricing decisions.

STEPS TO SETTING A COMPETITIVE TUITION RATE

Pricing tuition rates must bridge the relationship between posted price (advertised tuition rate), unfunded financial aid, and net tuition revenue. This relationship undergirds tuition revenue flow at nearly every institution, be it rich or poor. Tuition pricing strategies become counterproductive if they are applied willy-nilly and are not accompanied by a monitoring plan to track awards, enrollment, and net tuition revenue.

Several years ago before the recent round of tuition cuts to enroll more students, several tuition-dependent colleges substantially increased their unfunded aid; rather than enrolling more students, their enrollment fell and their net tuition tanked.[3] Their pricing strategy was a miserable failure. They had a plan but not a strategy. A strategy necessitates that consequences both good and bad are understood and that contingencies exist to limit damage. For these colleges, the strategy carried uncertain risks that could have been disastrous to their long-term viability. Pricing strategies, like other things sold in the market, have to be revised, adjusted, or abandoned when the market changes. Here are several components for developing a strategy with a proven track record in determining tuition rates, financial aid discounts, and net price to increase the probability that students with desirable characteristics will choose a particular college:

1. *Estimating Price Elasticity*—Regressions are used to estimate price elasticity for the book price (published tuition rate), the tuition discount rate, and the net price. The independent variables for the price elasticity regression include: degree

53

aspiration, achievement scores, income, and other variables relevant to the particular institution.

2. *Competitor Pricing Survey*—Assess the market for new students through a competitive set of colleges that compete for the same students. Examples of the variables used in the survey include: demographic characteristics of the students, current prices for the competitive set and the reference institution (the institution testing for new prices), and other relevant variables that have an influence on student choice and price.

3. *Pricing Matrix*—The regression parameters can be used to generate price points for the posted tuition rate, tuition discount, and net price. The matrix can be matched to probability of prospective student choosing a college at a particular price point.

BENEFITS OF THE PRICING SURVEY

The pricing survey can be used to assess whether (and how) the results may influence the design of the pricing study, as well as the recommendations for a pricing strategy going forward. A pricing survey can also be refined to help identify additional markets for particular programs that the institution chooses to explore. Finally, the survey can help confirm the pricing strategies for existing programs and the characteristics of existing markets.

ALTERNATIVE STRATEGIES

There are three primary pricing strategies to allocate financial aid based on the expectation that more aid will increase enrollment or attract a particular set with certain desirable characteristics. The first alternative strategy employs a financial aid grid; the second uses price as a proxy for quality, the third is crudely described as a trolling strategy. The elements of each alternative strategy are described below:

Financial Aid Grid: the grid arrays financial aid award according to the characteristics of the students sought by the college. For example, the horizontal axis may be arrayed by high school rank, and the vertical axis might be arrayed by the size of the award. Then, an expected award is assigned to each cell that intersects the horizontal and vertical axis by multiplying an average award for that cell with the target goal for the number of new students to receive the average award. As a rule, awards will increase with the scale of the academic measure.

The grid can also act as a monitoring instrument to track actual awards against the cell budgets. Table 13 is a sample financial aid grid.

Table 13

Sample Financial Aid Grid

High School Rank	Top 10%	11–20%	21–30%	31–40%	41–50%	51–70%	Totals
Awards							
70% of tuition	$50						$50
60% of tuition		$75					$75
50% of tuition			$150				$150
40% of tuition				$200			$200
30% of tuition					$400		$400
25% of tuition						$500	$500
Total Awards	$50	$75	$150	$200	$400	$500	$1,375

Price-Quality Strategy: Many private colleges employ a pricing strategy that targets the assumption held by students and parents that higher tuition rates are a proxy for quality. The proxy assumption seems to be related to the posted tuition at highly-respected institutions like Harvard, University of Pennsylvania, Stanford, or Duke. They then provide substantial tuition discounts to the best applicants. They signal quality by price, and convince students to enroll through deep discounts. Many middle and some lower-ranked colleges have used this strategy too. These latter institutions may alter the strategy by reducing the discount in order to generate sufficient revenue to cover ever-increasing expenses. Two conditions determine the effectiveness of the proxy pricing strategy for lower-ranked colleges. The first, condition occurs when sharp competition during a period like now of declining demographics force students to substantially increase the size of their discount. Under this condition, the financial well-being of the institution is put at risk. In the second condition, parents and students applying at middle- and lower-ranked colleges figure out that the price-quality proxy is not valid. In this case, the college is forced to fess up and make deep discounts to attract their new students.

Financial Aid Trolling Strategy: This strategy sees colleges offering tuition discount without any real strategy behind the discount or the offer. In many cases, these colleges confuse revenue with cash. That is, enrolling a student produces tuition revenue, but unplanned discounts can sharply reduce cash flows from tuition revenue. These colleges are simply acting like a recreational fisherman who throws a line in the water trolling for whatever fish will bite. In the case of the college, the admissions office throws out a line with an offer and hopes that a student will bite; i.e., accept and enroll. Trolling may work for a while, but it usually is linked to enrolling students without the academic skills to graduate, thereby increasing attrition rates and decreasing graduation rates. Strategic or operational errors in designing or implementing a financial aid program can have lingering and dangerous effects on the well-being of the institution. For instance, if the college awards students too much, the impact of over awarding students will diminish net tuition revenue (tuition revenue minus financial aid award) and cash flow from tuition over the several years in which the student is enrolled.

SUMMARY

Pricing strategy, in most cases, an institution sets multiple prices for different segments of its student market. Rarely do students pay the same price for their education as they are divvied up into desirable sets and priced accordingly. It is unusual for a student to pay full price regardless of wealth. Nevertheless, students willing or able to pay full price are like rare gems and are sought after because the institution gains the full cash value from the posted tuition. But colleges are unwilling to offer discounted inducements to attract these students outside of the reputed quality of their education.

As competitive pricing pressure ramps up, colleges will need to invest more time and resources to design effective pricing strategies. This chapter should help institutions consider the steps that they need to take to both design the strategy and to monitor their performance. Too many colleges have developed sophisticated financial aid strategies only to lose their effect when they are not monitored, and they inadvertently award too much aid. Mistakes in over-awarding financial aid can easily lead to multimillion-dollar errors that can push a college into a sizeable deficit that has lingering effects. The effects of financial aid errors linger because the awards have either explicit or implied long-term commitments to continue the same level of financial aid awards.

TAKEAWAY POINTS

1. Pricing is strategic and operational – strategic in that price needs to fit the student market for the college and operational in that the price needs to generate sufficient revenue and cash flow to cover a portion of expenses.
2. Pricing strategies have to take into account competitive markets and government regulations.
3. Pricing is most critical to tuition-dependent institutions; therefore, their tuition and discounts must be sensitive to student price elasticity. (If student markets are price elastic, major changes in price can result in loss of new students.)
4. Owing to the ease of transferring between colleges, pricing must not act as a mechanism to push new or on-going students into another college.

ENDNOTES

[1]   Melissa Korn, "A Study in Lowering Tuition," *The Wall Street Journal* (October 11, 2013): p. A3.

[2]   Scott Carlson, Goldie Blumenstyk, and Andy Thomason, "Enrollment: A Moving Target for Many Colleges," *The Chronicle of Higher Education* (October 18, 2013): pp. A2–A4.

[3]   JMA Higher Ed Stats, *Management Ratios: Private Institutions, xls: 1997–2000* (Boulder, CO: John Minter and Associates, 2002).

[4]   W. S. Reed, *Financial Responsibilities of Governing Boards* (Washington, DC: Association of Governing Boards and NACUBO, 2001): p. 3.

Chapter 6

Cost and Operational Performance

Colleges and universities are being pushed into a corner to reduce costs, increase graduation rates, and limit tuition increases—all at a time when governmental support is being cut. Most private colleges have responded to these pressures in an inchoate manner by focusing on increasing their unfunded institutional aid. However, there is a limit to how much institutions can increase unfunded scholarships because every dollar increase in unfunded aid is coupled to a dollar decrease in the cash generated from tuition. At some point, the college no longer produces enough cash to continue operations.

An alternative to increasing amounts of financial aid is for presidents and chief administrators to carefully analyze the cost and productivity of their operations.[13] The main question that they should ask is, "Are we producing graduates and services in the most effective manner?" This chapter will address this question through three approaches: basic contribution ratios, output-input ratio, and responsibility-centered management. The chapter ends with a brief discussion on the limits of external benchmarking of costs.

A major problem with analyzing cost and productivity in higher education is that accounting and administrative systems are typically not designed to collect the fine details needed for an analysis of operations. For example, the charts of accounts for many business offices are

---

[13] There are other alternatives to offset increases in financial aid, such as expanding enrollment, seeking out grants, and soliciting existing and new donors.

not disaggregated to specific activities within a department. It is not uncommon to find that these charts do not have detailed expenses or revenues by department or by majors. Moreover, performance analysis needs to understand the flow of students across majors as they take courses outside their assigned majors. If instructional costs or revenue are assigned only to majors where the students are housed, costs and revenue may either be overstated for the major department or understated for other departments providing instruction for a particular major.

This problem is solvable but labor intensive. First, it requires a new chart of accounts that lays out responsibility centers that will hold the expenses and revenue for all departments and functions that generate revenue. An example of those centers could be centers for each instructional department with a master responsibility center for all instructional departments or a center for athletics, or auxiliaries, or institutional development (fundraising). The responsibility centers for instruction will include tuition and fees minus unfunded financial aid, the direct costs (instructional and administrative), and indirect costs (general institutional costs). The president and chief administrators will need to agree on a set of algorithms to allocate indirect costs.

The second part of the solution to estimating cost and productivity depends upon the addition of variables to the administrative systems so that it reflects the responsibility centers and fine detail found in the chart of accounts. For instance, these variables will track as students move from admissions and through majors, course assignments, dormitories, food contracts, and student services. In addition, the administrative system should compile data on faculty assignments, contracts, class sizes, administrative contracts and responsibilities, and other relevant data. The purpose of the revised administrative variables is to permit tracking, costing, and productivity analysis.

Changes to the chart of accounts and the addition of new variables in the administrative system will differ by college. The redesign of accounts and systems is not an easy task, but the effort is worth it because the college will be able to more accurately estimate its costs of operation. These changes mainly fit requirements of the output-input ratios and responsibility-centered model (RCM) discussed below.

The advantage of cost and performance analysis is that the president and chief administrators can go beyond the broadsword cuts to programs or the jacking up of financial aid to compete in the market for students and can respond to governmental regulations. While reviewing the three methods of cost and operational analysis (contribution ratios, output-input ratio, and RCM), only the RCM provides specific targets for strategic intervention in an institution's cost and operational structure.

BASIC CONTRIBUTION RATIOS FOR EXPENSES AND REVENUE

There are two contribution ratio types, expenses and revenue, that depict the proportion of expenses reported for a department to total expenses and the proportion of revenue generated by a department to total revenue. These ratios are from either Prager, Sealy & Company's books on strategic financial analysis or from Moody's Investor Services monographs on credit analysis.

The *expense contribution ratio* relates a specific expense category to total expenses. The trend for those ratios will show if the distribution across expense categories (also called functions in accounting parlance) is changing over time. A larger share for an expense category implies that total expenses are also increasing if other expense categories are static or are also increasing by the rate of inflation.

1. General structure of the expense contribution ratio: expense function divided by total expenses. The expense function$_j$ comprises: instruction, student services, academic support, and institutional support. Indirect expenses such as: plant, depreciation and interest expenses are allocated to each expense function. Accounting rules require the indirect expenses to be

allocated according to a formula based on how the expense
may be employed by a particular expense function. Commonly,
plant expenses are allocated by square footage, while admission
expenses are allocated by academic majors.

2. Alternative structure of the contribution ratios: An alternative
   structure of the expense contribution ratio splits the expense
   function into payroll and nonpayroll expenses to determine
   relative growth of these factors for each function.

3. Benchmarking the expense ratio: The distributed expense
   ratios can be compared to different either internal or external
   benchmarks. An internal benchmark is a goal that the college
   sets for the distributed proportion of expenses for a particular
   function. An external benchmark compares the distributed costs
   of the institution to these types of third-party benchmarks: a
   competitive set of colleges, a standard for its Carnegie category,
   a value for its region, or a national benchmark. The external
   benchmark could be the mean, median, or other measure that
   the institution deems to be relevant.

The revenue contribution ratios are comparable in design to the expense
contribution ratios: the difference is that revenues for a particular
function are compared to total revenue. Like the expense ratios, the
revenue ratios are analyzed for changes over time. The institution
can compare both ratios to see whether the changes in expenses yield
more or less revenue over time. Nevertheless, these ratios are crude
approximations and do not provide sufficient information to draw
conclusions about the linkage between expenses and revenue.

OUTPUT-INPUT RATIO

An output-input rate is simply the ratio of the total outputs of the
institution (e.g., credit hours, degrees, patents, or other measurable
output) to the cost of the inputs (costs can be aggregate or severable,
such as payroll, material, or capital). The ratio indicates the cost of

producing an output. The challenge of output-input rates arises whenever an organization has multiple outputs and does not have a well-defined system for tracking outputs and their coincident costs (see the discussion of accounting for costs in the introduction to this chapter).

Measuring the chain of outputs and inputs for an institution requires sophisticated financial and administrative systems. Producing accurate output-input ratios requires that each output be tracked back to the set of costs that generated the output. A typical set of outputs includes credit hours, students, student skills, or degrees by major. The college produces credit hours; however, it does not produce students—although this is a measure often used in cost analysis in higher education. Degrees are supposedly the main output of the institution, but the question is how to measure the costs of producing the degree because most financial systems rarely, if ever, track input costs for a particular set of degree recipients over time.

1. General structure of the output-input ratio: $Output_j$ divided by $input_i$. $Output_i$ can be defined as credit hours by major, by degrees, or by major, by cohorts, by graduating class, by grants, by gifts, or by other measurable output. $Input_i$ is the cost of producing the $output_j$.
2. Data requirements: If the measure for output is degrees for a major, the college must be able to clearly identify the majors and the costs for producing the degrees of those majors during the period that they were enrolled and earning credits for the degree. This condition for data is true for other measures of output.
3. Benchmarks: There are no valid data on outputs given the data conditions stated above, and so the college could not make external comparisons. It would need to establish internal benchmarks for costs.
4. Productivity: The output-input ratio is a productivity ratio and as such could be used to manage both variables to improve productivity. Thus, costs could be identified and tracked to determine whether they are expanding faster than desired to produce the desired output. Also, the institution could manage

the process and time employed to, for example, improve the flow and speed for graduates to complete a degree. Since the output-input ratio can be used for cost control and productivity, it provides a powerful tool for managing the essential operational core that serves an institution's primary mission.

5. Strategic and operational intervention: The institution can use the output and input ratios to design strategies and operational plans to improve productivity. One way of targeting the output-input relationship is to subdivide the input variable ratios into the categories that generate the cost of operations. Here are several subdivisions of the input that can influence costs: output to labor hours, output to labor costs, output to material costs, output to capital expenses, or output to cost of technology. Subdividing the input ratio into factors should be done within the context of a trend analysis to see the magnitude of changes. In addition, the scale of each factor should be compared over time to which factor has the greatest influence on the sum of the factors for the input variable.

RESPONSIBILITY-CENTERED MANAGEMENT MODEL

Responsibility-centered management (RCM)[14], like the output-input ratio, is both a cost control device and a productivity tool. The central premise of RCM is the completion of the authority-responsibility circle by giving the faculty of schools or departments specific, measurable incentives to exercise their considerable authority responsibly for the benefit of themselves, their students, their organizational units, and the institution as a whole. RCM stipulates revenue and indirect cost allocation rules and then gives schools and other revenue-generating units the responsibility to cover the total costs of their programs (indirect as well as direct) from the revenues generated by their teaching, research, or business service activities. By plainly allocating the costs of facilities

---

14 This version of RCM is based on Stevens Strategy's adaption of the basic RCM model

and administrative services to the revenue-producing centers, RCM provides information on full program costs while focusing attention of the RCM managers on the quality and efficient production of their services.

The main requirements of the RCM model are data collection, specifying responsibility centers, and explicit allocation of full costs (direct and indirect costs) for each responsibility center. The biggest challenge with RCM is collecting cost and revenue data and assigning the data to the correct responsibility centers. Because students do not take all the courses within a single department, RCM sets out transfer pricing that takes into account the buying and selling of services between departments. As discussed below, the first step in pricing and cost allocation is to identify how credits are distributed across majors by using an induced course load matrix.[15] Once credit distributions are identified, cross-department (reasonability center) pricing can be established, and cost allocations can be made. RCM as a full-cost structure not only allocates the direct costs of the responsibility center, but it also allocates indirect costs to the responsibility centers. Indirect costs include academic support, student services, plant, depreciation, and interest.

The final revenue and cost allocations within the RCM model are summarized with the main revenue centers for revenue. Depending on the institution, those centers could include schools or academic programs, and revenue departments. A revenue department could be instructional departments, athletic programs, auxiliaries, development offices, or any other element of the institution that makes a major contribution to the net revenue of the institution. Lastly, there are usually a set of revenues that do not fit within a specific responsibility center, such as interest income, investment income, realized or unrealized income from investments, and other income that comes to the college but is not due to efforts of a particular center.

---

[15]   The structure and use of an induced course load matrix is available through ERIC at http://eric.ed.gov/?id=ED140708.

After the final allocations of revenue and costs, the RCM sums the net income produced by each responsibility center and those net revenues falling outside the purview of a center. The sum of net revenue should equal the net for operations reported in the audit or the final budgetary report for the current year. The audit becomes the benchmark for comparison of financial data within the RCM model.

Sam Preston, the Dean of the school of Arts and Sciences at the University of Pennsylvania, made the point that RCM compels "deans to determine their most valuable programs on both a qualitative and financial bottom line basis." Not only deans but all chief financial officers must come to grips with the implications of the outcomes of the results from the RCM analysis.

1. *Fundamentals of RCM:*
    a. RCM prescribes revenue and indirect cost allocation rules, assigning schools and other revenue-generating units the responsibility to cover the total costs of their programs (indirect as well as direct) from the revenues generated by their teaching, research, or business service activities.
    b. By explicitly allocating the costs of facilities and administrative services to the revenue-producing centers, RCM provides information on full program costs and brings to the attention of the institution and center administrators the quality and efficient production of these services.[32]
    c. Full costs are the sum of all variable and fixed resources used in producing a product or in rendering a service, including an appropriate allowance for physical asset depreciation and opalescence adjusted for any resale or salvage value.
    d. RCM allocates indirect costs to revenue centers based on established, simple, and understandable algorithms using the relative size and usage data. The algorithms should be understood, observable, and measurable by all institutional constituents.

e. An induced course load matrix is used in conjunction with RCM to identify the flow of credit hours across departments.

f. Depreciation costs must be part of any RCM model. Ignoring depreciation means that a major cost is ignored. By assigning depreciation to revenue centers, it plainly establishes the financial goal that a center must achieve to assure that the institution is a going concern.

e. When making comparisons of the RCM with the audit, the depreciation, interest, and other costs allocated to functions in the audit must be disaggregated.

2. *General Conditions to the RCM Model:*

   a. An induced course load is required to:
      i. Determine the flow of credits among responsibility centers
      ii. Estimate the average price per credit for pricing credits.

   b. Financial aid is allocated to instructional responsibility centers. This condition requires an accurate matrix for financial aid awards.

   c. Fees also need to be accurately allocated to the correct instructional responsibility center.

   d. Total tuition and fees net of financial aid should be reconciled to the audit.

   e. Institutional costs are allocated to responsibility centers based on the proportion of direct expenses allocated for instructional and noninstructional responsibility centers.

   f. Net income should be compared to the change in net assets for operations as reported in the audit.

   g. The RCM should be computed for multiple years so that trends, strengths, and weaknesses can be identified.

3. *Strategic and Operational Intervention:*

   Of the three forms of cost and operational performance management discussed here, RCM provides the best platform for strategic and operational plans that target the financial condition of the institution. Financial and operational strategies can be designed to target enrollment, tuition pricing (posted and discounted), the structure of academic programs, institutional development, athletic programs, auxiliary services, direct and indirect expenses, and capital expenses. As noted above, RCM requires a sophisticated data management system to collect and provide current and trend data so that the best point of entry for strategies and plans can be selected. RCM's benefits are worth the costs despite its demand on time, energy, and resources to keep it current.

There are four justifications for using RCM as a platform for analyzing and managing allocation decisions and operation performance. First, RCM closely reflects costs of operation within an institution. Second, RCM shows the relative performance of responsibility centers. Third, it reduces the tendency to assume that general education programs only provide services and do not generate income. RCM focuses the attention of the president and chief administrators on allocation decisions to strengthen success so that they can determine whether weak programs can be bolstered or need to be consolidated or terminated. If weak programs are not salvageable, then the decision is whether to reallocate their resources to stronger centers or to eliminate their costs entirely to improve the financial condition of the institution. (Refer to Appendix 6 for a fuller description of the model.)

LIMITS ON USING EXTERNAL BENCHMARKS TO COMPARE PERFORMANCE

External benchmarks as a tool for performance analysis should be used cautiously because their values are directly affected by the quality of the data and the unknowns regarding the nature of the institutions generating the data. Regrettably, IPEDS data is often the most problematic but is the primary benchmark in performance analysis.

One problem with IPEDS comparison sets is the consistency among institutions with the definition of a particular IPEDS variable. The second problem is the tendency of financial offices to shift departmental expenses to different expense functions[16] over a series of years. For example, some academic, administrative, and student services may be shifted to instructional functions to suggest that more is being spent on instructional programs. Shifting expenses among departments can have a deleterious impact on expense comparisons if the expenses being shifted are large enough to have a significant effect on distributions, ratios, and by implication comparisons.

The best way of dealing with these issues is to get a large enough set[17] of comparison institutions and compute the means or medians for each variable in the set. In addition, the analyst should have sufficient understanding of the institutions in the set to know how they are alike or different.

SUMMARY

Private institutions should take steps to convert their financial and administrative systems to produce the refined data needed to understand their costs, performance, and the relationship between the two. Current regulatory proposals suggest that a delay in upgrading systems will have an adverse effect on the capacity of a private institution to compete in the market for students. Late adopters will discover that they are making broad guesses about costs and do not have adequate information to improve allocation decisions and thereby manage tuition and fee changes. Colleges caught unprepared to compete on price will find themselves either unable to increase enrollment or, worse yet, losing students to their competitors.

---

[16] Expense functions group together a set of common expenditures, for example, expenses for instructional programs.

[17] A set of more than thirty will help to wash out some inconsistencies among the data.

TAKEAWAY POINTS

1. Given that cost drives tuition and fees often determine the revenue required to cover expenses, cost analysis should be a regular feature of operational analysis.
2. Operational metrics should include cost analysis metrics.
3. Costs need to be benchmarked against institutional goals or industry standards.
4. Financial, administrative, and academic data systems should be structured to collect the data needed for cost analysis.
5. Cost controls are a necessary element in managing tuition increases, competitive pricing, and efficiently allocating resources.

Chapter 7

Dashboards

The Voluntary Institutional Metrics Project has worked for two years designing a common dashboard for institutions of higher education.[18] The major problem with the project is that very few institutions have the data or the analytic tools to get at these measures. Very few colleges have the operational or financial data to determine what all degrees cost or the skills mastered, let alone the cost or skills for a particular degree.

Setting goals is simple, but having the capacity to achieve those goals is not. A goal like the cost of a degree appears to be a straightforward and achievable outcome on the surface, but it is soon overwhelmed by massive data issues. The essence of the problem in costing a degree is that colleges need to track the cost of a degree by student and by major. In most cases, administrative and financial systems do not differentiate associates, bachelors, masters or doctoral degrees. Redesigning a college data system to figure out the cost of a degree will cost a small fortune and will take an immense amount of time—neither of which colleges, especially small colleges that are struggling, have in abundance. Several

18 The Voluntary Institutional Metrics Project is a group of eighteen private, public, and for-profit institutions of higher education, which have joined together to design a common dashboard for higher education. The purposes of the common dashboard are to report: repayment and default rates on student loans; student progression and completion; cost per degree; employment outcomes for graduates; and student learning outcomes. The Project is sponsored by the Bill and Melinda Gates Foundation and was sponsored by HCM Strategists. HCM is a public policy and advocacy consulting firm specializing in health and education. The information on the Project and HCM came from the latter's website: hcmstrategists.com/analysis/voluntary-institutional-metrics-project/

presidents who participated in the project complained about the disconnect between project goals and the cost to generate the metrics to achieve those goals.

Dashboards are necessary and useful tools for presidents and boards of trustees. However, at this time, Project Dashboard may be too ambitious. Instead, key decision makers need a dashboard that provides a quick picture of the current and forecast condition of the college within its operating year.

PURPOSE OF DASHBOARDS

A dashboard is a template that reports on the trend for major variables that influence the financial condition of the institution or the performance of a division/department. A dashboard should also identify problems with an explanation on how the problems will be resolved. The dashboard should be timely and precise, and it should be a document that can be used as a reference for changing plans when performance is subpar.

MULTIPLE DASHBOARDS

Dashboards should be available to all departmental managers so that everyone is receiving daily information on the status of their particular responsibility plus a summary report of the status of the general condition of the institution. The design and implementation of the departmental dashboards may take considerable time, but the availability of information to recipient will aid in managing and problem solving. Below is a sample list of those who could benefit from dashboards:

1. Board of trustees
2. President
3. Chief administrative officers (design will vary by responsibility)
4. Budget department managers
5. Building and grounds

6. Auxiliary managers (design will vary by type of auxiliary operation)
7. Registrar, financial aid, and admissions (design will vary by responsibility).

HOW TO MANAGE WITH A DASHBOARD

The CFO, registrar, chief admissions officer, and human resource administrator should provide the data for the dashboard. The dashboard should be presented to the president, the cabinet, division leaders, and department chairs monthly, preferably within two weeks of the end of the reporting month.

Each level should focus its attention on:

1. Monthly: Variations between the budget and actual performance, or trends that could have an adverse impact on the financial condition of the college in the future
2. Academic Period end-of-the-year: performance for the period and on trends that could be adverse to fiscal year performance
3. Annually: Systematic reviews of performance to determine factors that had a major effect on performance. The annual dashboard review should be conducted in combination with an intensive review of all aspects of the institution.

It is in the interest of college leadership and their business offices to do the following to improve their ability to analyze performance.

1. Chart of Accounts: The chart should include every revenue-producing program and its attendant expense departments to accurately reflect the operational structure of the institution. In addition, expenses should be subdivided so that their impact on revenue production and on supporting operations can be identified and analyzed.

2. Assets and Liabilities: The chart should be designed so that it also reflects the revenue flow and expense department's operational structure of the institution.
3. Payroll: This system should complement the chart of accounts.
4. Depreciation and Interest: These should be allocated and updated to assign space and interest to the correct revenue and expense departments.
5. Enrollment System: The coding for enrollment by student and the coding in the chart of accounts should complement each other so that enrollments and financial accounts for each academic program can be aggregated and analyzed.
6. Reports and Analysis: Reports should analyze operation decisions and their effects. Annually, chief administrators should review the effectiveness of strategies, operational decisions, and instructional outcomes, marketing plans, capital investments, and financial performance. The institution should test ongoing, revised, and new strategies with its financial model.

SUMMARY

Dashboards are critical to managing strategies and operations. The purpose of the dashboard is to provide information to decision makers so that they can quickly identify problems that need to be addressed. It is imperative that dashboards are in the hands of decision makers in a timely fashion. A dashboard report is of little value if it arrives long after a problem has matured into a crisis.

TAKEAWAY POINTS

1. Dashboards should be a part of an operational reporting system.
2. Dashboards need to be:
   a. Easily understood by decision-makers
   b. Timely
   c. Pertinent
   d. Revised when new strategies or operational plans are put into place
   e. Redesigned when the information is not useful.

See Appendix 7 for sample institutional, division, and department dashboards.

CHAPTER 8

Salient Institutional Relationships

Achieving a state of financial equilibrium (building and sustaining financial viability) will depend upon salient relationships among people in key positions that can communicate, understand, design, and implement effective strategies and plans for financial equilibrium. Positions are salient when they have a direct and significant effect on budgetary and financial decisions. If chief administrators have the skills to work well with each other, there is a good chance that a college can achieve a state of economic equilibrium, or *ceteris paribus*. Conflict with one or more of these positions reduces the chance that the institution will have the financial management systems to respond to the massive economic changes facing it.

SALIENT POSITIONS FOR ACHIEVING ECONOMIC EQUILIBRIUM

The board of trustees, the president, and the chief financial officers are key salient positions because they shape the strategies, goals, responsibilities, and most routine activities associated with a strategic-financial management paradigm. These three positions have three important roles in the paradigm: development, affirmation, and validation. Development of a strategic plan is much more than sitting in front of an Excel sheet and entering numbers. It is an interactive application of authority that will determine the form and substance of financial strategies and plans. A plan without buy-in from the board, the president, and chief financial officer will be nothing more than a muddle.

Why is validation and affirmation an important aspect of the relationship among these salient positions in the paradigm? Validation is often critical prior to a decision and during the time when statutes, regulations, or other conditions require formal authorization by the board of trustees. Validation is often required for public institutions when they submit budgets for legislative approval, and for private institutions as part of a grant application or when they seek a publicly-backed bond or a bank-financed loan. Although the president or other chief adiminstrators may have the authority to act, their actions may not be considered legitimate by peers or subordinates without further validation by those positions above them, i.e., the board of trustees. Affirmation is a two-side coin that involves seeking approval from a superior in the institution even when approval is not required; and optimally it involves ascertaining the approval of subordinates to attain their consent to a decision. Affirmation is always a useful step to take in order to avoid future opposition that could stall the strategic or operational plans.

Among the top leaders, it is imperative that the president and the chief financial officer establish a mutually supportive relationship. It is in their self-interest to support the decisions and plans of each other if they want to achieve their institutional and financial goals. Of course, it is not judicious for either party, in particular the CFO, to make a decision without first acquiring mutual affirmation for the decision. There is nothing more upsetting to a president than to discover that the CFO has taken unilateral action, even if it is within the prescribed authority of the CFO—especially when the subject is sensitive to the mission of the college and/or to the president.

The CFO also plays an important role by being the proxy naysayer for the president. The implied understanding (but not formal duty) of the CFO is to say that some action cannot be taken because it violates policy, budgetary plans, or other authority of the business office. Although

though this duty can be distasteful to the CFO, it is imperative that she or he perform it so that the president can remain neutral and save his or her personal relationship capital for critical issue that affect the well-being of the college. In support of the nay-saying task, the president should acknowledge that the CFO has the authority to say no and that the president supports the decision without further argument. The aim is to make the CFO, not the president, the go-to person on budget and financial issues, policies, procedures, and requests. This practice can help the institution maintain the value of budget and business office policies, procedures, and plans. The practice is also in keeping with basic management theory that employees (in this case the CFO) have the appropriate authority and responsibility to perform their jobs.

The chief components of the salient relationship with the board of trustees and president are to inform, educate, and expeditiously prepare solutions. To inform is to provide immediate and clear information about the current financial conditions of the institutions and to describe any factors that could have a positive or negative influence on those conditions. Information is best relayed through a simple dashboard report. To educate is to explain complex financial transactions and reports in a fashion that can be understood by a layperson. Solutions require financial plans that respond to issues that the board or president wish addressed, such as changes in discount rates, debt financing, or employee benefits.

Because of the important responsibilities of the CFO, it is critical that the president and CFO have open, ongoing dialog to ensure that they are on the same page. The CFO must have a firm understanding of the institution's mission and the trustees' and president's vision for the future of the college or university.

SALIENT COLLEAGUE: MORE THAN THE PRESIDENT AND CFO

The paradigm will not work if only the board, president, and CFO are involved in the process because others within the institution have responsibilities and unique insights that can either strengthen the paradigm or lead to opposition if not consulted. Key salient colleagues should include the chief academic officer (CAO), the registrar, the chief admissions or marketing officer, and administrators from buildings and ground, information technology, and/or financial aid. Who is involved with paradigm decisions will depend on the type, context, and impact of a decision. Good salient relationships do not guarantee that there will be acceptance, that errors will be eliminated, or that strategies will foster economic equilibrium.

It is critical for the success of the strategy that the CAO and the CFO work in consort as they formulate financial strategies and plans. The CAO's contribution to the paradigm is the understanding this position has about the resources needed to achieve the academic mission. The CAO is also the main conduit for the budget process to the faculty. If the faculty perceives that the budget process is transparent and that the president and CFO understand the requirements and constraints of the academic mission, the faculty are more likely to support changes in financial strategies that have a direct impact on the academic program.

COMMON SET OF ECONOMIC AND FINANCIAL PRINCIPLES

Financial management must rest on the assumption that everyone involved in developing and managing financial strategy and budgetary plans understands and agrees that the institution operates under the constraints of a common set of economic and financial principles. If they do not agree, financial management will deteriorate into a continuing squabble over revenue sources, expense allocations, responsibilities, and the appropriate spending level for financial resources. These squabbles are not just sources of heartburn for everyone involved, but they also foster chaotic conditions in managing financial operations, which could also diminish the financial stability of the institution. Too often it is the loudest department, not the department that has a significant role in achieving the mission of the institution, that receives the largest share of the budget pie. Therefore, it is imperative that managers reach an accommodation on basic economic and financial principles. How agreement is achieved will depend on the unique characteristics of a specific institution. The basic principles noted below cover these areas at a minimum: economic forces, budget policies and rules, and essential accounting rules.

A COMMON GROUND ON ECONOMIC FORCES

The salient parties to the paradigm need to understand the markets that drive the financial conditions of an institution, such as students, gifts, grants, and labor. In each of these markets, the tension between demand, supply, and competition directly affects the price for what is being offered. For example, the number of students enrolling given the number of spaces available for enrollment will affect the price of tuition. Selective colleges will have greater control over their price, whereas nonselective colleges or colleges competing with other colleges for a limited market will have less flexibility in setting their tuition price. One way to resolve the tension between students' demand and colleges' supply of enrollment spaces is the size of the tuition discount offered. Over the past several years, the tuition discount among many lower-tiered colleges has increased as colleges fight to fill their enrollment slots.

The tension between demand and supply plays out in the market for gifts, grants, and labor (faculty, staff, and administration), as well. However, price may be determined by other factors than the offering of services. For example, gift giving may involve the value assigned to prestige, memories, culture, and the endearing qualities of the college in the memories of the alumni. Changes in prestige, policy, culture, or other characteristics of the college may diminish the college's value to an extent that the gift giver may not be willing to make the gift.

Grants have a more subtle pricing mechanism because the granting agency is buying the service and the reputation of the institution delivering the service. Grant markets are bounded by institutional reputation and the conditions imposed by a grantor. Given that grant markets are limited in size, most institutions will rarely be eligible for many of the available grants. Additionally grants (especially government grants) may include carrying costs, and institutions with limited resources may not want to incur the extra expenses required to administer the grants. Salient actors should include in their common understanding of economic forces the institution's position on grants. An institution can be thrown off its financial game plan by someone soliciting a grant that imposes conditions that result in costs greater than the dollar value of the grant or a grant that does not directly support the mission.

Supply and demand in the labor market and its impact on price (wages) is apparent to everyone who has sought a job. In higher education, like many organizations there are two labor markets, an internal market and an external market. Internal labor markets are used when positions are hired from within the institution. External labor markets come into play when positions are filled from candidates external to the institution. Pricing in a labor market depends on the number of people seeking a job. As the queue for a position expands, it restrains pressure to increase wages. On the other hand, as the queue shrinks, it puts upward pressure on wages. The best example is to watch how fast wages increase or decrease for technology positions when the demand shrinks or expands. Salient actors should know how the institution uses labor markets to fill its positions and how labor markets influence wage decisions.

If there is one source of discord among salient actors, it is with the concept of "scarce resources." Too often we wear blinders when it comes to expenditures and ignore that funds are scarce resources that limit what can be done. It would seem that many salient actors assume that funds are infinitely elastic, and can be expanded to whatever need is deemed important as opposed to eliminating activities that are no longer relevant but have a long history of being included in the budget.

The likelihood that scarce resources are ignored increases as planning moves down into the organization or away from positions that have to produce financial resources. This happens because either the position makes little or no contribution to the production of funds (revenue) or because the positions' budgetary responsibilities are so small that they do not see the larger impact of their requests on the budget or the finances of the institution.

A COMMON GROUND ON BUDGETS

Given the prevailing state of economic forces, the budget depicts the financial decisions that determine whether an institution can achieve economic equilibrium. In addition to a common ground on how economic forces shape financial decisions, the salient parties to critical financial decisions need to agree on the financial dynamics represented by the budget. For example, the enrollment flow dynamic (the main driver for tuition-dependent institutions) works as follows: revenue from enrollment follows a path the cost of admissions, to discounted tuition, to auxiliary revenue net of expenses, to the balance that is allocated to academic programs and student services. Anything left after academic and student service expenditures is allocated to administrative services, the plant, depreciation, and interest payments. The reality of the enrollment dynamic that everyone dealing with the strategic financial paradigm needs to recognize is that enrollment revenues barely cover the direct cost of instruction and academic services; that little is left for students services; and that nothing remains for administrative, plant, interest, or depreciation expenses. In other words, except for the very wealthiest of colleges, achieving economic equilibrium is a close-run thing at most colleges. It is only achievable if everyone—in particular the salient players involved in financial strategy and plans—can work together with a common understanding when formulating strategies, budgets, and general operational plans.

Essential Accounting and Business Office Rules

Few things have greater potential for upsetting the relationship between CFOs and nonfinancial managers than problems related to accounting rules. These rules constrain financial decisions and budget plans and, by implication, sanctions legitimacy of financial strategies and plans. An equilibrium strategy is almost worthless if the budgetary policies and procedures either do not exist or are regularly violated by nonfinancial managers.

In many institutions, accounting rules that regulate the value of restricted gifts and how they are allocated give rise to conflict between CFOs and nonfinancial managers. From the perspective of the CFO, setting accounting rules about gifts is a simple matter of referencing established policy by the Federal Accounting Standards Board (FASB). Many nonfinancial managers do not understand that the receipt of a pledge is not the same as the receipt of cash; neither do they understand that the use of restricted gifts is limited to the income generated by the gift and by the restriction imposed on the gift by the donor.

Although CFOs typically see accounting rules as a means of assuring that the business office complies with governmental regulations, accounting standards, and board policy, nonfinancial managers see these rules otherwise. To the latter group, accounting rules are maniacal instruments that undermine their freedom of action to solve real-world problems. Reaching common ground with nonfinancial managers on accounting rules is a difficult challenge to CFOs because both have different interests in the outcome of the financial game. Nevertheless, it is imperative to financial strategies, budget management, and hopefully economic equilibrium that the CFO and salient nonfinancial managers can come to an understanding about the rationale and benefits of accounting rules.

PRESIDENT'S FOSTERING OF SALIENT RELATIONSHIPS

There are several stipulations that the president must have in order to make salient relationships work. The first stipulation is that the president must hire the best people for key positions such as chief academic officer, chief financial officer, chief maintenance officer, chief enrollment and marketing officer, and chief information officer. Hiring the best people means that the institution will have to pay market rates for these positions, which will probably be above the historic rates for the institution. Getting the best people entails hiring candidates who have the skills and experience required for the position, and they need to have the personality to work well with the president and each other. Working well together does not require that the key officers act as a mere chorus of affirmations of whatever the president wants; neither does it require that a key officer accepts proposals from other key officers without comment. A team will work well together when the members are amenable personalities who can accept change, criticism, and the requirements that others must have fulfilled in order to succeed in their duties. Skills and working well with the president are fundamental to fostering salient relationships.

The second stipulation involves the president's willingness to trust the ability of key officers to do their work. Trust calls for forbearance in letting key officers do their work without the harassment or daily questioning of their judgment. Trust also sees the president providing the vision, goals, and plans to these officers so that they know the reasons for the actions that they are expected to undertake. Trust embraces the acceptance by the president that key players have legitimate reasons for saying no to some proposals.

The third stipulation is that the president must acknowledge the successes of these key officers. Acknowledging success does not necessarily require more pay or bonuses. Acknowledging success is also accomplished when the president tells peers and colleagues of their good work. Fostering salient relationships boils down to the president building a senior team who work well together, perform at the highest level, and agree to supporting the mission, vision, strategy, and plans for the institution.

SUMMARY

Salient relationships with the president, board, and colleagues are critical to the success of a new financial management paradigm. These relationships cannot be ignored and should be carefully considered during the development of strategic and operational plans. Here are several principles for building and maintaining salient relationship among the users of the financial paradigm.

1. Inform, educate, and respond to the board and president about financial plans and operations.
2. Work with colleagues who are critical to strengthening the financial condition of the institution and include them in:
    a. Operational meetings, which involve formal and informal meetings
    b. Budgetary performance reviews, to determine whether budget plans are on or off course and what can be done to resolve operational problems
    c. Budget and capital requirement planning, so that colleagues can provide their insight into ways of improving the allocation of resources and of identifying potential problems
    d. Establishing financial teams designed around important segments of financial or budgetary plans
    e. Reaching common agreement on economic forces that shape the financial condition of the college
    f. Working with nonfinancial managers so that they understand the rationale and benefits behind accounting and business office policies and procedures.

When it comes to the strategic-financial paradigm, the CFO is the key player in the development of financial strategies and operational plans. Even if the CFO is a skilled communicator (which is becoming a significant requirement for this position) and a competent accountant and financial manager, this should not lead to the conclusion that all problems will be eliminated in the relationship with salient colleagues. The reality is that CFOs, presidents, chief academic officers, and other chief administrative officers have different interests because the goals and processes of their positions push them away from accepting the basic demands placed on the office of the CFO. The best thing that a good CFO can do under these circumstances is to see issues that salient colleagues raise as opportunities and not as tribulations to be borne in disgruntlement and resentment. The latter makes for unhealthy relationships and an unhealthy lifestyle. It is comforting to know that most problems, when viewed in the rearview mirror of time, are often much smaller than when one is presently next to them.

TAKEAWAY POINTS

1. The president and chief administrative officers need to agree on financial strategies and the financial dynamics of the institution.
2. The CFO and president need to form a mutually supportive relationship.
3. The CFO should be prepared to become a proxy naysayer for the president.
   The purpose of the salient relationship with the board of trustees and the president is to inform, educate, and expeditiously prepare solutions.
4. Chief administrators and salient colleagues need to have a common ground and agreement about:
   a. Economic forces that affect the college's finances
   b. Budgetary dynamics
   c. Accounting processes and policies.

CHAPTER 9

Financial Management
of Online Programs

Colleges that are not delivering instruction online are learning that they are so far behind the curve that a significant portion of the student market is already lost. Adults are the largest component of new students in online programs, although a growing segment of online students are under twenty-five years of age. Moreover, the rate of increase for new students in online programs is outpacing students enrolling in brick-and-mortar colleges. The problem for colleges that are late entries into the online market is that the low-hanging fruit and the big net revenue returns are gone. Late arriving colleges to the online market are left with market niches that do not have the revenue potential that was available to early entrants to online markets.

This chapter delves into the financial management of online programs by offering insight into the cost of the general structure of the online program, the cost of delivering instruction online, marketing costs, tuition-pricing budget models, and any budget controls that are essential to the success of these programs. There are four sections: general operational structure, cost of a learning delivery system, marketing costs, tuition pricing, and budget models.

GENERAL OPERATIONAL STRUCTURE

The college should organize its online learning program as a separate academic department or as part of the evening or adult degree programs with the capabilities for: marketing, learning delivery, budget management, and assessment.

A strong leader of the department, who can develop a competitive program and manage its resources with responsibility for strategy, implementation, and oversight of the programs, is an imperative. The online manager will have the main responsibility for getting the program up and running. During the first two years, the manager should perform such basic tasks as: setting up learning programs, scheduling classes, hiring faculty, contracting for a learning management system (LMS), marketing, coordinating with the information technology department, advising students, and overseeing the budget. As enrollment and net income expands, the online manager will need to allocate extra resources to hire assistant managers to oversee daily operations.

The online department manager needs two skilled managers: a program designer and a marketing/admissions officer. The program designer should have the experience to install and support an LMS. The marketing/admissions officer should have considerable experience designing effective marketing and enrollment campaigns. Faculty should have classroom experience, at a minimum; preferably, they also should have taught online classes.

A successful online program is determined by the skills and experiences of the online management team. The institution will need to pay market rates if it wants the best person for each role. Market rates could easily exceed the standard rates for comparable positions in the institution or the local labor market. Nevertheless, a skilled team can shorten the learning curve for starting the online program. A good team could produce significant financial benefits by the end of the second year. However, if the institution hires an inexperienced team, and they have to develop their skills on-the-job, the learning curve could be long and costly. The worst outcome for a new online program is an inexperienced team that fails to grasp the complexity of their work, resulting in firing and hiring new teams every year, which will postpone positive income production for years.

The compensation costs of the online management team can vary widely. These cost ranges can guide the online program team during the development of the budget

1. Online manager range: $85,000 to $110,000 (The upper end of pay could be 50% greater subject to the experience and success of the candidate.)[1]
2. Learning designer range: $58,000 to $61,000[2]
3. Marketing/admissions officer range: $85,000 to $100,000[3] (This position is overpriced because the institution needs to hire a person with proven experience developing a successful marketing campaign and with experience or knowledge about admissions procedures.)

Some of these positions may already be filled by staff in an existing adult or evening program.

Another structural decision is whether to employ full-time or adjunct faculty. Compensation and benefit costs for full-time versus adjunct faculty are different and subject to institutional policy. The costs that need to be considered include training for online instruction, using the learning management system, course preparation, recording grades, and payments for faculty who design curriculum or courses that are used by other faculty. (The institution should review the American Association of University Professors policies on course content development and ownership before developing a policy on these issues for their online program.)

Table 14 is an organizational chart showing the basic positions needed to deliver an online learning program. The administrative team (online manager, marketing/admissions officer, program designer), and full-time faculty, if any, represent the largest portion of fixed costs for the program and have a major impact on tuition rates.

Table 14

Basic Online Program Organizational Chart

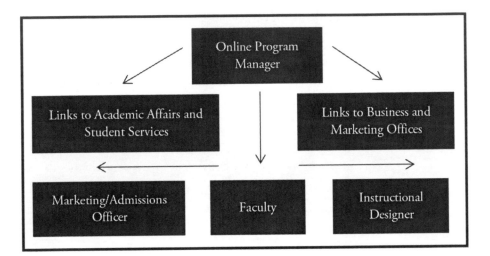

While it is in the interest of the online program to hire the best personnel, it is also in its interest to minimize expenses. If expenses are not controlled, then the cost of operations as enrollments increase could easily overwhelm revenue production. Higher costs mean more students are needed to reach a financial breakeven point. Of course, during program development and implementation of a new online program, costs will be high; however, these costs and their impact on balancing revenue against expenses should be anticipated in the budget.

Finally, depending on the rules of the particular regional accreditation commission for the institution or any requirements by special accreditation or regulatory authorities, there may be additional costs imposed upon the online program. Added costs may flow from state and proposed federal regulations requiring an institution to be accredited or certified by its own regional accrediting commission and state higher education authority and by the respective accrediting commission and state authority in each state where it enrolls students.

COST OF A LEARNING DELIVERY SYSTEM

There are usually three options for delivering online instruction: using existing institutional online courses or curricula, subcontracting online instruction, or developing new online learning courses. Online instruction, like an institution's classroom instruction, must be valid and effective; anything less is unethical, damaging to the student, and compromises the integrity of the college. The following sections provide information on the major components in delivering an online learning program.

Online Hardware

Online programs rely on their operational technology to deliver, manage, and provide learning services. There are three hardware components in an online operating system: a communication network, server space, and links to external learning resources such as the library. The communication network manages data flows between and among: students and faculty, the librarians, information technology help desk staff, and other support or administrative staff within the institution. Since online programs absorb a tremendous amount of server memory and hard drive capacity, the system should be sufficiently robust to store: the LMS (if housed by the institution), video programs, and additional space to allow for two years of double-digit enrollment growth. Although excess server capacity is expensive, an online program does not want to be caught short by a spurt in enrollment that would thwart increases in net income generated by the program. Online programs need to build student academic and computer support so that students can readily resolve academic questions and problems in using the LMS. These programs should strive to minimize student aggravation and frustration caused by long delays in responding and solving online service problems.

The information technology department can help the program manager identify the hardware needed to build a robust system. Finding the right hardware can take time; but if it is done with due diligence, it is worth time and associated cost of the search. The business office can also assist in figuring out the initial and annual allocation of hardware cost to the online program.

Software

Online programs need an "LMS" to coordinate and manage course delivery. The prime vendors for these systems are Blackboard, Moodle, and Angel (many other LMS vendors are available). Two options are available to online programs regarding an LMS; they either purchase the software and place it on their system or they contract with the vendor to house the software on its hardware. The advantage of using a third-party vendor to house the software is that they provide the servers and maintain the IT support to keep the system up and running. For smaller institutions, this is a tremendous advantage because it reduces the capital investment of purchasing the hardware to store the LMS. One major consideration in the purchase of an LMS is whether it integrates and is compatible with the institution's administrative software.

The college should never assume that it will remain with one vendor forever. LMS records should be kept on-site, subject to security procedures, for accreditation reviews, and to protect its own interest if the vendor closes or is sold to another company.

Colleges do not necessarily have to contract with their own faculty to design courses. There are a large number of vendors for online course modules; the program administration will need to search the web, talk with directors of other online programs, and get in touch with a national association for online programs. Modules usually come with the text software and the capacity to feed back to the LMS.

Massive open online courses (MOOCs) are an alternative course delivery system that is delivered by an outside vendor. However, the use of MOOCs for course credit will require careful review of legal and accreditation complexities.

Typically, the start-up cost for an LMS system that hosts approximately five hundred students or the equivalent number of credits earned by five hundred students is somewhere around $50,000 with annual costs of about $15000-$25,000 (these are rough estimates of the costs where the contractor hosts or holds the software). Annual costs will increase in increments above the student limit, with incremental costs usually diminishing as the enrollment increases.

Assessment

Since most regional accrediting commissions and institutions of higher education require assessment of academic outcomes, the cost of assessment should be part of the budget. The budget decision involves determining whether to conduct an assessment using in-house resources or contracting with a third-party contractor to develop an assessment package. Additionally, the cost of designing an online assessment package depends on how well the online instructional program aligns with the institution's classroom instruction and assessment methods.

MARKETING COSTS

Online education is a highly-competitive market with such well-known brand names as Southern New Hampshire University, Wilmington University in the Mid-Atlantic region, Argosy College in Colorado, and many nationally-known colleges and universities.

Thus, an institution new to the online market should expect to spend a considerable amount of money to get its name known in the marketplace and to convince students to enroll. Unfortunately, large expenditures do not end with enrollment of the first students because marketing costs will grow to keep pace with the market and to increase enrollment.

The institution's web page is the main marketing device for recruiting online students. The program should spend the money to make it easy to use, assure linkage to search engines, and use key words to improve its chance of being listed on a prospect's search list. A web address that is buried deep in a search list is nearly worthless. It is, therefore, in the interest of the college to not stint on the design of a website and the relevant support services to keep the site up and running. Creating effective websites is not inexpensive. For example, a reputable third-party contractor will have a minimal charge somewhere in the range of $125,000 to $150,000. If the college intends to get its money's worth, the college should thoroughly test the website under expected operating conditions.

In addition to an effective website, the program needs a targeted campaign that reaches a larger geographic area than is already served by the college. This campaign should inform prospects about the program and convince them to contact the college. The program should expect to pay an experienced vendor about 10 percent of estimated tuition revenue to design and run a target message campaign.

The cost of the advertising program will vary by the cost of designing advertisements and by the intensity of the campaign. Ad design cost depends on whether ads are prepared in-house or by a third party. Campaign intensity is determined by the cost, location, and frequency of placement of the ads. Placement costs usually depend on the number of clicks on the web advertisement—specifically, the college should look for click-through charging schemes. The click-through scheme charges the advertiser when a prospect does more than open the ad; the advertiser is only charged when the prospect actually goes to the website.

In summary, the marketing budget should expect to spend:

1. For start-up: up to $150,000 to design a new institutional website, or it could be lower if the vendor is only designing the online component for an institution's website
2. For targeted messages: 10% of the expected revenue
3. For other advertising:
    a. Start-up: $50,000
    b. Ongoing advertising: range from an initial start-up cost of $50,000 up to $200,000 or more depending on the rate of growth specified in the program's enrollment goals.

TUITION PRICING

Tuition pricing may be determined three ways: the online tuition charge by competitors, institutional pricing policies, or a simple breakeven model with a competitive pricing goal. Institutional pricing policies vary too much to hazard a recommendation based on a standard policy so this section will only deal with competitive and breakeven pricing.

Online Competitive Prices

An online program manager should know the tuition prices and pricing strategy of the competition. Competitive pricing and strategy should inform the pricing strategy of the program by setting a price benchmark and by delineating the program's strategy for responding to its competitors' pricing strategies.

Here is how the program manager can identify its competitors' pricing and pricing strategies:

1. Identify the main competitors and their prices within the geographic reach of the online program's market.
2. Identify key elements of the pricing strategy, for example: targeted discounts, price differences by programs, and rates of changes in pricing.

Breakeven Pricing

Breakeven pricing is a method for identifying the minimum price for breaking even with the cost of operation. The cost of operation can include a rate for net income, which may range from 50% to 80% of program expenses depending upon institutional policies on returns expected from revenue-generating academic programs. Breakeven prices should be compared to the competitions' tuition prices. If the price is in excess of the competition, the cost structure or rate of net income will have to be reduced. If the net is reduced substantially, the value of the income flows from the online program to the institution's bottom line could be compromised.

Here is a basic formula and guideline for computing breakeven pricing:

1. BEP = ((FC+VC) * (1+r)) / X
   a. BEP is the breakeven price
   b. FC+VC: FC are fixed costs and VC are variable costs; FC+VC are the total operational expenses for the fiscal year
   c. X is the total forecasted enrollment
   d. r is desired rate of net income

2. As noted above, the institution should be leery of reducing the net income rate (r), and it should consider the performance impact of inflating enrollment forecasts.

BUDGET MODELS

Before delving into budget models, note that although the financial condition of online programs is in a constant flux, they still must maintain a state of "equilibrium." Recall that the chapter on Economic Equilibrium stipulated that equilibrium is the condition when positive changes in net assets generate sufficient cash flows to increase cash balances to achieve and support the mission over the long-term. The online program should support its own economic equilibrium and contribute sufficient resources to the economic equilibrium of the institution.

BUDGET CONDITIONS

Two budgets are necessary when considering an online program. One is a start-up budget, and the second is the operating budget. The following list sets out several conditions that need to be considered during the development of the start-up or operational budget.

1. Strategic goals for the program, such as enrollment, cost of operation, and change in net assets
2. Marketing goals, advertising plans for each academic period, and associated expenses
3. Enrollment forecasts by academic period
4. Tuition rates and financial aid discounts, if any (because tuition for most online programs is already heavily discounted, they do not need to offer additional tuition discounts)
5. Cost of course and degree program development, such as payments to faculty or others developing courses or contract payments to an outside vendor for course development

6. Faculty (full-time and adjunct) assignments and costs by academic period

7. Detailed staffing requirements, expenses, and responsibilities

8. Capital strategic goals that establish measurable outcomes for capital equipment, such as the number of students served by the equipment and limits on equipment downtime

9. Capital expenditures and the costs of operating the equipment

10. Cost of compliance with relevant governmental and regional accrediting regulations

11. Costs for conducting program assessment

12. Design of the operating and budget performance reports at the end of each academic period

13. Design of variance budget reports through the end of drop-add periods to show significant and unexpected changes in fixed and variable costs.

Budget Templates

Three templates follow which are useful in budget controls: a start-up budget, an operating budget, and a variable performance report form. These templates are only models and should be adapted to the institution and to its current conditions. It is imperative that the online program allocates enough money to advertising and marketing, especially during the start-up phase when the college is trying to build its brand. Also, the operating budget should include the change in net assets and cash generated from operations. Financial performance that only focuses on changes in net assets ignores the very real need of the college to produce sufficient cash to cover its liabilities, to build its reserves to respond to emergencies, to expand operations in response to demand, and to meet its equilibrium requirement to have sufficient reserves to support its mission.

Table 15

Start-Up Budget Template

Budget Item	Budget Amount
Administrative, Staff, and Full- or Part-Time Faculty Compensation Costs	
Employee Training Costs	
Course and Assessment Development Costs	
LMS: Capital and Operational Costs	
Online Program Website Development Costs	
Marketing and Advertising Costs	
Capital and Non-Capital Equipment Costs	
Software and Software Support Costs	
Administrative and Instructional Supplies	
Accreditation and Government Regulatory Compliance Costs	
Total Start-Up Costs	

Table 16

Operational Budget Template

Budget Item	Budget Amount
Net Tuition Revenue	
Expenses	
Administrative, Faculty, and Staff Compensation and Benefits Expenses	
LMS Expenses	
Hardware and Software Expenses	
Advertising and Marketing Expenses	
Accreditation and Regulatory Compliance Expenses	
Non-Capital Equipment Expenses	
Interest and Depreciation Expenses	
Other Expenses	
Total Expenses	
Change in Net Assets	
Net Cash Flow	

The variable performance report should be completed after the end of the drop-add period. This report should be sent to the chief financial officer. In addition to the variable performance report, the program manager should prepare a performance report at the end of each academic period and at the end of the fiscal year. The purpose of this report is to compare actual performance to budget expectations and to identify problems that need to be addressed during the next period or fiscal year.

Table 17

Variable Performance Report

Item	Budget	Actual	Variance
Enrollment			
Net Tuition			
Learning Expenses			
Other Variable Expenses			
Unplanned Expenses (List)			
Net Variance			

Summary

It is all too apparent that online programs are becoming a major component in an institution's net income flow towards its bottom line. Colleges behind the online curve could find their bottom line adversely affected as its competitors sweep new students into their marketing net. A college seeking to make a big splash in regional or national online markets must come to terms with the cost of marketing in a large online market space. Rather than entering a large or national online market, it may be more prudent initially for a college to enter a market circumscribed within its existing geographic area, especially if the institution already has an established evening or adult degree program. The preceding discussion about online market finances may assist the leadership of the institution in making a reasonable decision about entering the online marketplace.

TAKEAWAY POINTS

The main takeaways for a new online program:

1. Conduct a thorough due diligence study of the: costs, regulations, methods of operation, marketing campaigns, and obstacles to success before initiating an online education program.
2. Precision in financial management is everything.
3. Continuous oversight of finances is essential.

END NOTES

[1] CUPA (2014) Unweighted Median Salary by Carnegie Classification; 2014 CUPA-HR Administrators in Higher Education Salary Survey" http://www.cupahr.org/surveys/ahe-surveydata-2014.aspx

[2] CUPA (2014) Unweighted Median Salary by Carnegie Classification; 2014 CUPA-HR Professionals in Higher Education Salary Survey" http://www.cupahr.org/surveys/phe-surveydata-2014.aspx

[3] CUPA (2014) Unweighted Median Salary by Carnegie Classification; 2014 CUPA-HR Administrators in Higher Education Salary Survey" http://www.cupahr.org/surveys/ahe-surveydata-2014.aspx

CHAPTER 10

Field Guide Final Notes and Thoughts

This book addressed financial strategies, operational plans, and management tools needed by institutions as they respond to massive changes emanating from new regulatory regimes, financial markets, and competitive forces. These changes are pushing institutions away from the pure nonprofit model that has traditionally characterized financial management in higher education. The new financial model looks very much like a for-profit model in which the significant issues are cash flow, asset growth, profit, management ratios, and index measures of performance, not unlike the ratios used in business. Moreover, the financial system is expected to quickly generate financial data in real time and to be in the hands of the president and chief administrators. They do not want it later; they want it now so that they know what is happening operationally and whether they need to reconsider the short-term and long-term goals of the institution.

If leaders wait for financial pressure to mount before they begin to consider how their institution should address structural change, they may find that their institution is in financial jeopardy. The effect of structural changes will hit both private and public institutions; even rich private institutions have found that changes in financial markets can have a devastating effect on their current income flows. In addition, the past decade has proven false the assumption that publics are somehow insulated by state funds and also reap substantial gains from the economic forces that adversely affect private colleges and universities. The result is that institutions, no matter where they are in the higher education market, must be prepared to address structural changes:

As higher education moves toward a quasi-for-profit model of financial management, the governance system of institutions remains fraught with ambiguities that confound the speed and financial methods needed to respond to massive changes taking place. The ambiguities in leadership follow from the split in authority between faculty, boards of trustees, and the president. Because there is no unified governance structure in most institutions, the president and chief administrative officers will need to be adept at maneuvering new strategies through the institution. The strategic planning system that Stevens Strategy has been using with colleges over the last dozen years has proven particularly adept at producing the consensus or at least the understanding to adopt and implement new strategies. It is the coupling of strategic consensus with the financial strategies and management tools proposed in this book that will prove most valuable to the institutions that are ready to find their way through the complexities facing them.

This book provides institutional leaders with these models to respond to the fast-paced changes hitting their institutions.

> *Financial Paradigm* offered a new method of managing the financial condition of an institution by encompassing all components of its financial structure (refer to Chapter 1).

> *Equilibrium Model* provided a model for achieving and managing financial equilibrium, which is the point where financial resources are able to sustain the mission of the institution (refer to Chapter 2).

> *Financial Health* described several models for measuring the financial condition of an institution and for developing strategies to strengthen financial health (refer to Chapter 3).

> *Forecast Model* suggested parameters for designing a sophisticated budget forecast model (refer to Chapter 4).

> *Pricing and Discounts* discussed how to effectively set tuition rates in highly competitive markets and in response to potential government regulations (refer to Chapter 5).

Cost Management laid out methods for analyzing and managing operational costs (refer to Chapter 6).

Sample Dashboards explained how dashboards can deliver important data needed to understand and to manage operations at all levels in an institution (refer to Chapter 7).

Salient Relationships considered the network that needs to be created within an institution to assure that it achieves it strategies and carries out its operational plans (refer to Chapter 8).

Financial Management of Online Programs provided basic rules for the financial management of online programs (refer to Chapter 9).

Due Diligence Checklist includes major items to consider when assessing operational performance (refer to Appendix 1).

Diagnostics Checklist has five major components for assessing strategic performance: governance, academics, markets, finances, and management of operations (refer to Appendix 2).

Variable Budget Report provides a format for analyzing variable revenue and expenses during the fiscal year to determine if the institution is meeting its operational budget goals (refer to Appendix 3).

Strategic Options for Financially-Struggling Colleges suggests strategies when a college faces economic and financial pressures beyond its control (refer to Appendix 4).

Sample CFI Template has a sample template for the standard computation of the composite financial index (this template often changes; revisions are published in newer editions of *Ratio Analysis in Higher Education*; refer to Appendix 4).

Responsibility-Centered Management Model sets out the steps for entering data into the RCM matrix.

> *Dashboards* provide several different performance dashboards for the president and for other chief officers (refer to Appendix 7).

SURVIVAL AT THE BRINK

Before I conclude the book, I want to offer several insights on strategies for colleges and universities that are trying to survive at the brink of survival. As The *Wall Street Journal* reported in late 2013, enrollment at more than a quarter of private universities fell more than 10 percent, with enrollment at some colleges falling by more than 17 percent, from 2010–2012.[1] According to The Journal, declining enrollments are the beginnings of long-term shift toward smaller admission pools. The article notes that enrollment peaked in 2008 and that enrollment will decline for the balance of the decade. Their findings tie into earlier studies by the Department of Education, which also found that these declines will be heaviest in the Northeast, Mid-Atlantic, and most of the Midwest.

The Journal suggests that middle-tier institutions with low endowments and high tuition rates are the most vulnerable because enrollment declines are being amplified by "new technologies driving down costs and profit margins, rising student debt, a soft job market for college graduates, and stagnant household incomes."[2] The Journal believes that the preceding factors presage a shakeout "that will reorder the industry."[3]

Stevens Strategy believes that well-run colleges and universities can survive the shakeout. However, there will be instances when even the best-run institution is trapped by circumstances that are inescapable and will demand drastic action. This chapter offers three strategic approaches for dealing with impending threats to financial stability from lower enrollments and more intrusive government regulations of tuition rates. The strategies reflect institutional responses to initial pressures on its financial viability to options in response to conditions that threaten the survival of the institution. More suggestions about survival at the brink are in Appendix 4.

Survival Strategic Approach #1: Comprehensive Strategic Review

The first approach is taken when the college forecasts a series of deficits that will require extraordinary action to turnaround. A comprehensive strategic review has two purposes: determine the current condition of the institution and formulate strategic turnaround plans. The strategic condition of the institution is assessed by analyzing data about its finances, academic programs, operational cost structure, and markets. Following the collection and review of data, the analysis then identifies the institution's strengths, weaknesses, threats, and opportunities. The development of turnaround strategies involves specifying opportunities in terms of programs and net income, selecting several of the strongest opportunities, and developing detailed plans for implementation. Conducting a comprehensive strategic review will embrace all sectors of the institution so that each sector understands the reasons for the turnaround, the conditions for the turnaround, and expectation that they are to contribute to the turnaround.

The strategic plan may yield a variety of options such as: "right sizing" the institution, outsourcing some departments (food services, bookstore, public safety, custodial services, etc.), incentive separation packages, new markets, new programs, new athletic teams, and new gifts or grants, etc. Furthermore, the strategic plan can focus on reallocation of expenditures that better fit the mission of institution. All options are worthy of considerations that can promise either a significant increase in revenue or to decreasing expenditures subject to the mission of the college.

One strategy that has been underutilized so far and is controversial among some academic leaders and that is to use online instruction delivered to traditional students. There are a variety of reasons why this group of students may choose online courses. First, they may want to speed the completion of their traditional program through a mix of traditional classroom and online instruction. Second, although they want a four-year degree, they are not comfortable in a traditional classroom setting. Third, they may want or need to combine work and earning a degree. Fourth, they may have been home schooled and prefer a learning environment where they have more control over the structure, pace, and intensity of their instruction.

Survival Strategic Approach #2: Form Strategic Alliances and Partners

The second approach that is worthy of consideration whenever an institution has reported consecutive deficits over several years, and the deficits have begun to erode the financial resources of the institution yet have not left it bereft of resources. This approach uses components of the first strategy and focuses on forming alliances or partnerships with other institutions. The concept is to expand revenue markets, to increase scalability of costs, and to eliminate redundant costs. This strategy will cause the loss of some freedom for the institution because they will have to work through a joint decision process. Nevertheless, it offers a college a better chance of surviving this troubled decade.

Survival Strategic Approach #3: Mergers

The third approach results when a college has reported consecutive deficits, their DOE scores have resulted in letters imposing sanctions on the college, their accreditation is at risk, and lenders have notified the college that it has failed to comply with its loan covenants. This approach rests on the comprehensive, strategic review of the first approach. The difference is that the strategies focus on merging with a stronger institution while it keeps its name and a semblance of its history within the new entity. Usually this step must take place quickly before the college's financial and operating conditions become untenable.

Survival Strategies—Final Thoughts

The preceding strategic option and the prior option have been common in industry to strengthen their position or to survive. When a product a product or service is no longer differentiated in the market, buyer choices are made solely on competitive variations in price. For many small institutions that are tuition dependent (be they public or private), price competition (i.e., price wars) is a threat to their ability to generate sufficient revenue to fund themselves. The ability to generate revenue and more importantly in terms of daily operations, cash is diminished as price competition leads to ever larger tuition discounts, resulting in reduced production of net revenue and cash. Partnerships and mergers become inevitable for survival under these circumstances as the survival of the institution becomes more doubtful.

Over the past three decades, colleges have sidestepped predicted demographic and financial catastrophes. The best example of their nimble response to demographic changes was the end of the baby boom market in the early 1980. Many commentators prophesied that these dismal demographics would extend over several decades and would eventually force fifty percent of private colleges to fail. Their sturm and drang prophesies did not come to pass because colleges developed the adult market and, in particular, encouraged women to earn or complete degrees that had lain fallow for several decades. The strategy worked and private colleges prospered. Now, we have to see if colleges are still nimble enough to survive the new demographic crisis exacerbated by prospects turning away from a college degree because it costs too much.

The evidence according to *The Wall Street Journal* and the Department of Education suggests that hunkering down and ignoring the future is not a strategy that will assure the survival of the college. Nevertheless, private colleges can survive, but it will take strategic plans that are supported by vigilance, leadership, and incorporate shrewd financial plans. *See Appendix 4 for more options that are available to struggling colleges.*

SUMMARY

This Field Guide drew on sources that we believe will provide chief administrators, in particular the president and chief administrative officers, with the strategic financial that they will need to adapt their institution to the demands of this dramatic historical period in higher education. These changes will have a significant influence on markets, competitive forces, the cost of instructional services, and the size of scope of their institutions, as well as on the financial resources required to respond to these changes. I believe that with foresight, good analysis, well-designed strategy, and the tools suggested herein, an institution can successfully navigate the troubled waters that lie ahead.

There is one point that this book wants to stress: waiting for more agreeable demographics, economics, government programs, or accreditation standards is no longer feasible. Presidents, boards of trustees, and the faculty must come to grips with the reality that they have to reduce the cost structure and/or the price of attendance at their institutions. Reducing costs and tuition will require new strategies and operational plans to make the institution more competitive in price, programs, and operations. To reiterate, the dynamics of higher education are going through a dramatic paradigm change, and delay in taking the steps suggested by this book could threaten the sustainability of an institution.

TAKEAWAY POINTS

1. Financial management is more than producing a positive net income. It must incorporate management of income flows through the statements of activities, financial position, and cash flow.

2. Economic equilibrium is a financial state that is evident when an institution can fulfill its mission with adequate quantity and quality by maintaining the purchasing power of financial resources and maintaining facilities in satisfactory condition.

3. The financial health of an institution should be assessed annually and the findings used in the development of strategies, operational plans, and budgets.

4. Financial forecasting models should be sufficiently robust and sophisticated to allow a broad range of financial plans, such as compensation plans, new departments' net income, or capital financing projects.

5. Pricing is strategic and operational – strategic in that price needs to fit the student market for the college and operational in that the price needs to generate sufficient revenue and cash flow to cover a portion of expenses.

6. Given that cost drives tuition and fees and forces the amount of revenue required to cover expenses, cost analysis needs to be a regular feature of operational analysis.

7. Dashboards need to be clear, concise, timely and pertinent.

8. Chief administrators and salient colleagues need to have a common ground and agreement about:
   a. Economic forces that affect the college's finances
   b. Budgetary dynamics
   c. Accounting processes and policies.

END NOTES

[1] Douglas Belkin, "Private Colleges Squeezed," *The Wall Street Journal* (November 9–10, 2013): p. A1.
[2] Douglas Belkin, "Private Colleges Squeezed," p. A5.
[3] Douglas Belkin, "Private Colleges Squeezed," p. A1.

APPENDIX 1

Due Diligence Checklist

Table 18

Due Diligence - Operational Performance Checklist

1.	Corporate or Institutional Documents	
1.1	Articles of incorporation or legislative charter	
1.2	Organization by-laws	
1.3	Corporate or organizational minutes	
1.4	Certificate of good standing	
1.6	All state or local business licenses or permits	
1.7	Organizational enabling legislation	
2.	Accounting Review	
2.1	Audited financial statements for the last three years	
2.2	Monthly financial statements for the last 18 months	
2.3	Management letters for the last three audits	
2.4	Capital expenditures for the last 3 years in categories	
2.5	Capital expenditures for the current fiscal year	
2.6	Budget projections for the current fiscal year	
2.7	YTD financial statement with prior year comparison	

2.8	Schedule of deferred maintenance	
3	**College Operating Data**	
3.1	Last 3 years tuition and fee history	
3.2	Last 3 years enrollment history—new and returning	
3.3	Last 5 years annual student census	
4	**Advertising and Marketing Data**	
4.1	Yield and conversion ratios for five years	
4.2	Advertising expenditures by media type	
4.3	Yield rates by media	
4.4	Yield rates by admission officer	
5	**Miscellaneous**	
5.1	Copies of reports used to manage the college or university	
5.2	Current tuition earnings report by student	
6	**Tax Review**	
6.1	Past three years tax returns	
6.2	Payroll tax reports—past three years	
6.3	Correspondence with federal or state tax authorities	
7	**Contractual Relationships**	
7.1	Any articulation agreements	
7.2	Advertising, marketing, and public relations agreements	
7.3	Service or maintenance agreements of any type	
7.4	Agreements with suppliers or vendors	
7.5	Existing outstanding purchase commitments and surety bonds	

APPENDIX 2

Diagnostics Checklist

**Use these diagnostic tables to guide
strategic and management reviews.**

Table 19

Financial Diagnostics-Operations

	Check Off
1. Is the operating net or total net increasing or decreasing; if it is decreasing, why?	
2. Are revenue and expense growth rates in balance?	
3. If revenue is falling, why?	
4. What is the trend for net tuition price relative to expense growth—rising, falling, or stagnant?	
5. What is the trend for net tuition revenue relative to expense growth—rising, falling, or stagnant?	
6. What proportion of revenue is gifts?	
7. Do auxiliaries produce a positive net income?	
8. If the expenses are growing faster than revenue, why?	
9. Is the growth rate for core expenses less than for noncore expenses; if so, why?	
10. What is the trend in total compensation?	
11. What is the tuition dependency rate?	
12. How does operational performance compare to the competition?	

Table 20

Financial Diagnostics-Operational Drivers

1.	What is the enrollment—by level and by program?	
2.	What is the attrition rate—by level and by program?	
3.	What is the graduation rate—by level and by program?	
4.	How many employees—faculty, staff, and administration?	
5.	What is the cost of employees—faculty, staff, and administration?	
6.	What is the allocation of employees allocated between core and noncore services?	
7.	What is the student-faculty ratio?	
8.	What is the average class size?	
9.	How many classrooms are there?	
10.	How is space allocated between core and noncore services?	
11.	How many parking spaces are there?	

Table 21

Financial Diagnostics-Working Capital

1.	Are cash and short-term investments increasing over time?	
2.	Are cash and short-term investments growing as fast as expenses?	

3.	What is the source of the increase in cash?
	   a. Is cash being produced by extending payables and accruals?
	   b. Or, is new cash being produced by adding short- or long-term debt?
	   c. Items 3 a, b, and c indicate that cash reserves depend on special circumstances to provide operating cash reserves.	

4	Are cash and short-term investments greater than 16 percent of expenses (a rough measure of one month of cash disbursements from expenditures)?	
5.	Are receivables as a proportion of tuition increasing; if so, why?	
6.	Are uncollectible accounts as a proportion of receivables increasing; if so, why?	
7.	Are students billed monthly?	
8.	What is being done to collect outstanding bills?	
9.	Is inventory as a proportion of auxiliary sales increasing; if so, why?	
10.	Are payables and accruals as a proportion of expenses increasing; if so, why?	
11.	Are vendors, taxes, and benefits paid on time?	
12.	Is short-term debt increasing; if so, why?	
13.	Prepare a short-term debt list—terms, lender, payment schedule, and reasons for borrowing.	
14.	Is the available funds ratio (cash and short-term investments to current liabilities) declining; if so, why?	

Table 22

Financial Diagnostics-Long-Term Capital

1.	Is long-term debt increasing?	
2.	List for long-term debt—terms, conditions, payment schedules, and uses? (Include all forms: on- and off-balance sheet borrowing.)	
3.	Is the debt leverage ratio less than 2:1? If so, debt may be excessive.	
4.	Does the college have a debt policy?	
5.	Is the return on net assets declining; if so, why?	
6.	Is the capitalization rate less than 50 percent? If so, it may limit future borrowing.	

7. How does the return on investments (endowment) compare to a benchmark (e.g. S&P 500)?	
8. What is the investment policy of the college?	
9. What is the payout ratio for the endowment fund?	
10. How is the payout ratio computed?	
11. Is there deferred maintenance? If so, how much is it and list the major categories.	
12. Is there a long-term strategy for space utilization for the campus?	
13. Does the college have sufficient parking?	
14. Are new facilities designed and located to permit sale?	

Table 23

Financial Performance
(Place reports in a three-year trend table.)

1. Have weights and growth rates for revenue and expenses been computed?	
2. Has the five-year trend in operating cash been reviewed?	

3. Have these ratios been computed?
  a. Tuition dependency
  b. Net tuition after unfunded institutional aid
  c. Operating margin
  d. Cash income
  e. Cash expense
  f. Current ratio
  g. Uncollectible receivables
  h. Payables and accruals
  i. Viability
  j. Debt service
  k. Interest expense
  l. Composition
  m. Capitalization
  n. Age of facility	

o. Free expendable resources to operations p. Total financial resources per student q. Endowment payout	
4. Compute the preceding ratios for the previous five years and compare trends.	
5. Is the primary ratio less than .40? (A ratio less than .40 means that the college may not have the capacity to transform itself or to cover five months of expenses.)	
6. Is net income with depreciation less than 2 percent of total revenue? (If so, this suggests that the college is living beyond its means and may not be building adequate reserves.)	
7. Is the viability ratio less than 1:1? (When this ratio falls below 1:1, a college's ability to respond to adverse conditions from internal resources is jeopardized. The ratio should fall in the range of 1.25–2.0.)	
8. Compute the CFI score for the college.	

Table 24

Financial Distress-CFI Score < 3

1. Conduct a strategic analysis of the college.	
2. Is the current market viable? Why do students choose or not choose the college?	
3. Can the institution produce new revenue or cut expenses to survive? a. Are there new sources of revenue? b. Can costs be cut through reorganization? c. Can the college run a fundraising campaign? Who are the benefactors? d. What is the condition of the plant? e. Can debt be refinanced or reduced through gifts?	
4. What is the college's strategic turnaround plan?	

Table 25

Major Financial Distress-CFI Score < 1

1. Is the CFI score < 1?	
2. Has the state warned that licensing will be withdrawn?	
3. Has the US Department of Education imposed financial conditions before student aid can be received?	
4. Has an accrediting agency warned that accreditation will be withdrawn?	
5. Does the college have sufficient cash or other investments to pay its bills?	
6. Can the college meet its payroll?	
7. Are payroll tax payments delinquent?	
8. Are payroll benefits delinquent?	
9. Is the college delinquent on debt payments?	
10. Has the college considered a merger?	
11. Does it have a survival/turnaround plan? Is it feasible?	
12. Has the college declared financial exigency?	
13. Is there a viable plan to close in an orderly fashion?	

APPENDIX 3

Variable Budget Report

Table 26

Variable Budget Report

Notes
1 The *variable budget report* tracks significant budgetary and performance variances during the fiscal year.
2 Send variable budget reports to the president and chief administrators at the end of each academic period.
3 Variable budget reports require subsidiary enrollment, section, and tuition budgets by academic period.
4 Expenses should include major operating expenditures that are growing faster or slower than expected.

	Current Academic Period			Year-to-Date		
Basic Variable Drivers	Budgeted	Actual	Net	Budgeted	Actual	Net
Enrollment						
Sections						
Financial Aid						
Revenue Variances						
Net Tuition						
Other Revenue						
Changes						
Total New and Variable Revenue						

Expense Variances		
Added Sections		
Unbudgeted Positions		
Unbudgeted Salary Increases		
Added Taxes		
Added Benefits		
Total New Expenses		
Other New Expenses		
Total New and Variable Expense		
Total Net Changes		

Appendix 4

Strategic Options for Financially-Struggling Colleges

Here are several options that a financially-pressed college may want to consider.

1. Change the investment mix to increase the portion of cash so that it can avoid short-term loans or selling equity investments in down markets.
2. Explore the option of a sale-leaseback of the campus or a portion of the campus to payoff bonds or other long-term debt. If there is any excess from the sale, it could be used to set up a strategic reserve.
3. Eliminate or cut back administrative and staff positions that do not directly contribute to recruitment and marketing.
4. Cut out low-priority perks such as cars, expense allowances, conventions, or other trivial activities that do not lead to the production of income.
5. Postpone all major capital projects.
6. Reallocate space within and among buildings, redesign class schedules, and reorganize administrative services to empty one or more buildings. Empty buildings could then be rented.
7. Use employees and volunteers (for example, students, alumni, and other interested parties) to run fundraising campaigns during evenings and on weekends.

8. Package off-campus properties and offer them to real estate developers.

9. Outsource as many service functions as possible, such as administrative and academic computer systems, the bookstore, public safety, payroll department, custodial and maintenance services, and food services. Even specialized student support services like tutoring, counseling, and health services should be considered for outsourcing. (Some outsourced services may pass back to the institution after the crisis passes or as part of a larger strategic plan.)

10. Redeploy assets to support productive revenue generating programs.

The list is not exhaustive. Rather, it is suggestive in that it shows there are many ways to deal with financial problems. Although the options in this list are not difficult to implement, they do require the will to act early and decisively. Too often key leaders waste early and opportune time to halt the slide into financial instability. Once the moment passes, reserves may have been drained, and the college may no longer be salvageable.

Appendix 5

Sample Composite Financial Index Template

Table 27

Sample Composite Financial Template

Example of a CFI Scoring Goal: Achieve a Score of Three or Greater		
Primary Reserve	**Formulas**	**CPI Values**
add unrestricted net assets	from audit; add	1
add temporarily restricted net assets	from audit; add	1
subtract property, plant, equipment (net of depreciation)	from audit; subtract	2
add long-term debt	from audit; add	3
numerator = total expendable net assets	sum	2
denominator = total expenses	from audit	10
Ratio =	compute ratio	**0.20**
Net Operating Revenues		
numerator = change in unrestricted net assets from operations	from audit	10
denominator = unrestricted operating revenue and operating reclassifications	from audit	10
Ratio =	compute ratio	**1.00**
Return on Net Assets		
numerator = change in net assets	from audit	10

denominator = total net assets (beginning of year)	from audit	10
Ratio =	compute ratio	**1.00**
Viability		
add unrestricted net assets	from audit; add	1
add temporarily restricted net assets	from audit; add	1
subtract property, plant, and equipment (net of depreciation)	from audit; subtract	2
add long-term debt	from audit; add	3
numerator = expendable net assets	sum	2
denominator = long-term debt	from audit	3
Ratio =	compute ratio	**0.67**
CFI Scoring Sheet—Institutions with Long-Term Debt		
Primary Reserve	(primary/.4) * .35	0.18
Net Income	(net income/.02 * .1	5.00
Return on Net Assets	(primary/.06) * .2	3.33
Viability	(primary/1.25) * .35	0.19
CFI Score		**8.70**

APPENDIX 6

Responsibility Centered Model (RCM) Rules

This appendix includes a detailed description of RCM and includes several tables illustrating the structure of various parts of the RCM matrix.

1. General Structure of the RCM Model:
   a. Net income for instructional responsibility centers: Net Income$_i$ = Direct Revenue$_i$ +/- Transfer Revenue$_{ij}$ - Direct Cost$_i$ - Indirect Cost Allocations$_i$, where i = a single instructional responsibility center, and ij = the transfer of revenue between instructional center$_i$ and other instructional centers$_j$.
   b. Net income for other responsibility centers: Net Income$_k$ = Direct Revenue$_k$ - Financial Aid - Direct Cost$_k$ - Indirect Cost Allocations$_k$, where k = a single, noninstructional responsibility center.
   c. Sum of net income for all responsibility centers: Total Net Income = $\Sigma_{i,j\ ...,\ n}$ (net income).

2. Set up an induced course load matrix. Here are the basic rules for cells.
   a. The columns hold the credit hours that students took in courses offered by the particular program. The sum at the bottom of the column represents the total number of credit hours earned by students in courses offered by the academic program.

126

b. The rows, when summed, are the total credit hours earned by students who selected the majors included in the program.
c. This is an example of a distribution of credit hours:
  i. If a student is in the business academic program, and six credits are earned by the student by taking two business classes offered by the business program, then six credits are entered in the cell where the column "Business" crosses the row "Business."
  ii. If a student is in the business academic program, and six credits are earned by the student by taking two liberal arts classes offered by the liberal arts program, then six credits are entered in the cell where the column "Liberal Arts" crosses the row "Business."
  iii. Here is a sample of an induced course load matrix illustrating the preceding examples:

Table 28

Induced Course Load Matrix

Academic Program	Business	Health	Liberal Arts	Total
Business	6		6	12
Health				
Liberal Arts				
Total	6		6	12

3. Data sources for the induced course load matrix includes:
   a. Audited financial statements
   b. Unaudited administrative data: enrollments, sections, and contracts are reconciled to budget annual reports, and then are reconciled to the audited financial statement.

4. The revenue calculations for the induced course load matrix are:
   a. An average tuition rate is computed by dividing total tuition revenue (per the annual budget report by program

after reconciliation with the audit) by the total credit hours for the year.

b. Tuition revenue for each revenue center is computed by multiplying the credit hours in the cells of the induced course load matrix by the average tuition rate; this will generate a second matrix with tuition revenue.

c. Fees are allocated. (How? Some examples are according to graduates by program, or new students by academic program.)

d. Grants and gifts are assigned to the development function if they are unrestricted or not designated for research.

e. Auxiliary income is assigned to the auxiliary function.

f. Other revenue sources that are not associated with a responsibility center are listed below the net income computations for the responsibility centers.

5. Financial aid is allocated by credit using an average financial aid per credit (total financial aid divided by total credits). The average is then multiplied by the credits in cells of the induced course load matrix.

6. Net tuition is the difference between total tuition revenue and financial aid in each cell of the induced course load matrix.

7. Direct expenses:

a. Direct expenses are the total expenses assigned to a department.

b. Departments are aggregated by function; for example, instruction includes the instructional departments, the auxiliary departments, the development departments, etc.

8. Physical plant, depreciation, and interest expenses are allocated:

a. First, by square feet per school

b. Second, by credit hour per academic program.

9. General and administration expenses are allocated according to the following rules.
    a. First, determine the proportion of direct expenses allocated to instructional centers and the proportion allocated to noninstructional centers.
    b. Second, determine the proportion of credit hours for each instructional center; then multiply the credit hour proportion and the proportion of indirect expenses for instructional centers to get the indirect expense allocation for each instructional center.
    c. Third, determine the proportion of direct expenses for each noninstructional center; multiply that percentage with the total indirect expense allocation for these centers to produce the indirect cost allocation for the noninstructional centers.

10. Student services are allocated by credit hour by school.

11. Revenue center analysis matrix:
    a. Revenues
        i.   Net tuition is aggregated by school by function
        ii. Noninstructional departments are summed by department and by function.
    b. Expenses are totaled for direct, physical plant, depreciation, interest, direct support, general and administration, and student services for each center.

Table 29

Sample Revenue Center Analysis Matrix

Function & Schools	Net of Total Revenue (A)	Direct Expenses (B)	Plant (B)	Depreciation (B)	Interest (B0	Direct Support	G&A (D)	Student Services (D)	Total Indirect	Net Revenue
Arts		minus	minus	minus	minus	Total A & Bs = C	minus	minus	Total Ds = E	C minus E
Sample	8	2	1	1	1	3	1	1	2	1

APPENDIX 7

Dashboards

Table 30

President's Dashboard Set

Summary Financial Report						
	Current Fiscal Year Budget			Fiscal Year-to-Date Comparisons		
	Year-to-Date	Budget	Variance	FY 1	FY 2	FY 3
Revenue						
Tuition and Fees						
Grants						
Gifts						
Auxiliaries						
Other Income						
Total Revenue						
Expenses						
Instruction						
Student Services						
Academic Support						
Institutional						
Auxiliaries						
Other Expenses						
Total Expenses						
Change in Net Assets						
Cash Balances						
Debt Principal						
Uncollectible Receivables/Tuition						

Capital Projects—Cash

	Cash Received	Disbursed	Balance
Project #1			
Project #2			
Project #3			
Project #4			
Project #5			

Enrollment—Headcount

Categories	Current Fiscal Year Budget			Fiscal Year to Date Comparisons		
	Year-to-Date	Budget	Variance	FY 1	FY 2	FY 3
Total						

Enrollment—FTE

Categories	Year-to-Date	Budget	Variance	FY 1	FY 2	FY 3
Total						

Enrollment—Full-Time Students

Categories	Year-to-Date	Budget	Variance	FY 1	FY 2	FY 3
Total						

Enrollment Part-Time Students

Categories	Year-to-Date	Budget	Variance	FY 1	FY 2	FY 3

Total						

Total Credit Hours

Categories	Year-to-Date	Budget	Variance	FY 1	FY 2	FY 3
Total						

Total Admission Report

	Current Fiscal Year Budget			Fiscal Year-to-Date Comparisons		
	Year-to-Date	Budget	Variance	FY 1	FY 2	FY 3
Inquiries						
Applicants						
Accepted						
Deposits						
Enrolled						
Matriculated						
Average Test Score						

Undergraduate Admission Report

	Year-to-Date	Budget	Variance	FY 1	FY 2	FY 3
Inquiries						
Applicants						
Accepted						
Deposits						
Enrolled						
Matriculated						

Tuition Discount Percentage						
Average Test Score						

Continuing Education Admission Report

	Year-to-Date	Budget	Variance	FY 1	FY 2	FY 3
Inquiries						
Applicants						
Accepted						
Deposits						
Enrolled						
Matriculated						
Average Test Score						

Total Sections

	Current Fiscal Year Budget			Fiscal Year-to-Date Comparisons		
Categories	Year-to-Date	Budget	Variance	FY 1	FY 2	FY 3
Total						

Average Class Size

	Current Fiscal Year Budget			Fiscal Year-to-Date Comparisons		
Categories	Year-to-Date	Budget	Variance	FY 1	FY 2	FY 3
Total						

Retention						
	Current Fiscal Year Budget			**Fiscal Year-to-Date Comparisons**		
Categories	Year-to-Date	Budget	Variance	FY 1	FY 2	FY 3
Total						

Graduation						
	Current Fiscal Year Budget			**Fiscal Year-to-Date Comparisons**		
Categories	Year-to-Date	Budget	Variance	FY 1	FY 2	FY 3
Total						

Total Counts by Category						
	Current Fiscal Year Budget			**Fiscal Year-to-Date Comparisons**		
	Year-to-Date	Budget	Variance	FY 1	FY 2	FY 3
Administration						
FT Faculty						
PT Faculty						
Staff						
Student-Faculty Ratio						

Total Employee Pay						
	Current Fiscal Year Budget			**Fiscal Year-to-Date Comparisons**		
	Year-to-Date	Budget	Variance	FY 1	FY 2	FY 3
Administration						
FT Faculty						
PT Faculty						
Staff						

Total Employee Benefits						
	Current Fiscal Year Budget			Fiscal Year-to-Date Comparisons		
	Year-to-Date	Budget	Variance	FY 1	FY 2	FY 3
Administration						
FT Faculty						
PT Faculty						
Staff						

Standard Measures						
	Benchmark or Goal	Year-to-Date		FY 1	FY 2	FY 3
Revenue/ Employee						
Cost/FTE						
Cost/Matriculant						
Marginal Revenue/Student						
Marginal Cost/ Student						
Revenue/ Expenses						

Table 31

General Institutional Dashboard

	FY:	Month:			
	Budget	**Actual**	**Variance**	**Prior FY**	**Est June 30**
Summary Financial					
Revenue					
Expenses					
Change in Net Assets					
Admissions					
Undergraduate					
Masters					
Doctorate					
Total					
Enrollment Headcounts					
Undergraduate					
Masters					
Doctorate					
Total					
Sections					
Undergraduate					
Masters					
Doctorate					
Total					
Average Class Size					
Undergraduate					
Masters					
Doctorate					
Total					
Credit Hours					
Undergrad					
Masters					
Doctorate					
Total Credit Hours					
Attrited					
Undergraduate					
Masters					
Doctorate					
Total					

Bibliography

Adelman, C. *The Toolbox Revisited: Paths to Degree Completion from High School to College.* Washington, DC: US Department of Education, 2006.

Belkin, D. "Private Colleges Squeezed." *The Wall Street Journal,* November 9–10, 2013, p. A1.

Carlson, S., G. Blumenstyk, and A. Thomason. "Enrollment: A Moving Target for Many Colleges," *Chronicle of Higher Education,* October 18, 2013, pp. A2–A4.

Cave, M., S. Hanney, M. Kogan, and G. Trevet. *The Use of Performance Indicators in Higher Education.* London: Jessica Kingsley Publishers, 1988.

CUPA (2014) Unweighted Median Salary by Carnegie Classification; 2014 CUPA-HR Administrators in Higher Education Salary Survey" http://www.cupahr.org/surveys/ahe-surveydata-2014.aspx

CUPA (2014) Unweighted Median Salary by Carnegie Classification; 2014 CUPA-HR Professionals in Higher Education Salary Survey" http://www.cupahr.org/surveys/phe-surveydata-2014.aspx

Cyert, R. *The Management of Universities of Constant or Decreasing Size.* Public Administration Review, July–August 1978.

Dehne, G. *Student Recruitment: A Marketing Primer for Presidents.* Old Saybrook CT: GDA Integrated Services, 2001.

JMA Higher Ed Stats. *Management Ratios: Private Institutions, xls: 1997–2000;* Boulder, CO: John Minter and Associates, 2002.

JMA Higher Ed Stats. *Management Ratios 2002: Private Colleges, Universities, Catalog #3690103.* Boulder, CO: John Minter and Associates, 2003.

JMA Higher Ed Stats. *Strategic Higher Education Trends at a Glance: F2 2002.csv and F2 2007.csv Financial Data.* Boulder, CO: John Minter and Associates, 2008.

Korn, M. "A Study in Lowering Tuition," *The Wall Street Journal,* October 11, 2013, p. A3.

Reed, W. S. *Financial Responsibilities of Governing Boards.* Washington, DC: Association of Governing Boards and NACUBO, 2001.

Ruger, A., J. Canary, and S. Land. "The President's Role in Financial Management." In *A Handbook for Seminary Presidents,* edited by G. Lewis and L. Weems Jr. Grand Rapids, Michigan: William B. Erdman Publishing Company, 2006.

Salluzzo, R. E., P. Tahey, F. J. Prager, and C. J. Cowen. *Ratio Analysis in Higher Education,* fourth edition. Washington, DC: KPMG and Prager, McCarthy & Sealy, 1999.

Strauss, J. and J. R. Curry. *Responsibility Centered Management Lessons from 25 Years of Decentralized Management.* Washington, DC: National Association of Colleges and University Business Officials, 2002.

Townsley, M. K. "Brinkmanship, Planning, Smoke, and Mirrors." *Planning for Higher Education* 19, no. 2 (summer 1991): pp. 7–32.

Townsley, M. K. "A Strategic Model for Enrollment-Driven Private Colleges," *Journal for Higher Education Management* 8, no. 2 (Winter/Summer 1993) pp 57-66

Townsley, M. K. "Deficit Prevention: Budget Control Model for Enrollment Dependent Colleges." In *Business Officer.* National Association of College and University Business Officers, October 1994, pp. 40–44.

Townsley, M. K. *The Small College Guide to Financial Health* (second edition). Washington, DC: National Association of College and University Business Officers, 2003.

Townsley, M. K. "Leveraging Facilities for Competitive Advantage; Essay 5." In *Presidential Perspectives,* edited by M. Fennell and S. Miller. Philadelphia: Aramark, 2007.pp 1-5

Townsley, M. K. *Strategic Turnaround Toolbox.* Washington, DC: National Association of College and University Business Officers, 2007.

Townsley, M. K. *Weathering Turbulent Times.* Washington, DC: National Association of Colleges and Business Officials, 2009.

Zemsky, R. and P. Oedel. *The Structure of College Choice.* New York: College Entrance Examination Board, 1983.